In Search of Musical Excellence

Taking Advantage of Varied Learning Styles

by
Sally
Herman

Acknowledgment

Most sincere gratitude and appreciation to Scott Foss, my editor, for his patience, encouragement, and tireless effort spent on this book. Not only were his suggestions invaluable, he also was a very positive force. This positive attitude and sharing of expertise helped make writing this book a very rewarding experience. It was exciting to witness the devotion with which this man approaches his craft.

Foreword

Sally Herman, a master-teacher and a consummate musician has, at last, shared her expertise through a book that is not just to be read – but to be studied and used as a daily guide for successful teaching of choral singing.

Her recommendation to "narrow down concepts with a few simple rules" is good advice to which she herself has adhered within the contents of this book. Beginning with a reminder that music educators are not entertainers, Sally has structured her text so that the reader will benefit instantly from a study of the first few pages and, furthermore, discover a continuum of methods which will ". . .guarantee a higher level of performance."

That the Kiersey and Bates book "Please Understand Me" had a strong influence on Sally is evidenced by the emphasis she places on ". . .understanding personality temperaments and learning styles" of students. Their findings are expertly summarized and clarified by Sally who provides a coherent set of guidelines which choral directors will find most beneficial in their attempts to ". . .instill feelings of success" within their students.

One of Sally's fundamental convictions is to ". . .teach the students in a manner so that they have no need for us." In Chapter 3, she has described just how we might proceed to accomplish this. Here she as narrowed down the elements of musical expression to a discussion of dynamics, diction and articulation. Outlined with ". . .few simple rules," one finds practical techniques which will attract students with ". . .different learning styles." These engaging and informative suggestions give us a glimpse of the personal procedures which have made Sally Herman the master teacher she has become.

Not being one to prescribe to "quick fixes," Sally speaks as much to and about the ". . .teacher's expanding personal horizons" as she does about the student or the choir. Although her mission to "instill feelings of success" is directed toward the student, it is my opinion that by practicing the methods offered in this book it is the teacher who will experience invaluable "feelings of success."

Because Sally Herman has a national reputation as a teacher/clinician/conductor and has achieved tremendous success within her own classroom, I believe that her concepts and methods should be studied by everyone who is "IN SEARCH OF MUSICAL EXCELLENCE."

Eph Ehly, DMA
Conservatory of Music
University of Missouri – Kansas City
1993

Table of Contents

INTRODUCTION

What is the most exciting choral performance that you have ever experienced? Why does that performance remain memorable to you? Most memorable choral performances are achieved because the choir attains a level of artistry that the listener characterizes as an "emotional experience" rather than a performance.

Think for a moment about the extraordinary performances that have remained in your own memory bank. Certainly, beautiful tone and precision are among the important ingredients of a quality performance, but without the finesse of artistically executed phrases, the listener is left with the feeling that something is missing. All of these qualities need not be indigenous to the professional or mature choir. The very young singer can be taught to sing with great artistry as is evidenced by the many wonderful childrens' choirs in this country and abroad.

For most of us, the opportunity to work with a highly select choir is rare. Most of our choirs are built around scheduling conflicts and too little rehearsal time. By presenting concepts to the singer in simple, clear terms and showing the singer how to implement those concepts, any choir can greatly improve performance quality. Because there is so much to teach, narrowing down concepts becomes imperative. If we can teach beautiful, artistic phrasing with a few simple rules, we stand a much better chance of reaching a remarkably higher level of musicianship with our students.

Many choirs find it difficult to "live" with a piece long enough to develop the musical understanding of the score needed to attain a high level of artistry, which necessitates finding more efficient use of rehearsal time. Because we often teach our students each piece, note by note, they do not develop a sense of musical understanding that will allow them to make judgments about shaping phrases in a new score. Once we establish this as our method of teaching, our students depend on us for all musical decisions, especially the young singer. Our task as a teacher is to give students the skills to make their own musical decisions. Robotics has a place in the automobile industry, but not in the choral performance industry.

Sometimes it is difficult to remember that we are music educators and not music entertainers. Because we are subjected to rigid performance schedules, we try to get those performances prepared as quickly as possible in order to meet all obligations. "Quick fixes" often are substituted for taking time to "educate" as we are preparing a performance and we easily become addicted to the "quick fix" method of teaching. "Quick fixes" are not necessary if we make every minute of class time as efficient as possible and teach our students to make many of their own musical decisions.

To make our students dependent on us for musical decisions is like being the over-protective parent. It takes patience to allow the toddler to slowly walk to the car and climb up into the seat. It is so much faster and easier to simply pick him up, carry him to the car, and place him in the seat. Likewise, it takes self-discipline as a teacher to allow our students to learn for themselves through experimentation and application, but *the best gift we can give our students is to teach them to not need us.* For this gift we gain their love and respect.

Because the area of musical performance is so intangible, the challenge of presenting it clearly in an educational setting where you serve a majority of the students, becomes an enormous task. Much research has been done on learning styles and how teachers can be more effective in the classroom with a better understanding of how learning styles are different. An understanding of the types of personality temperaments and learning styles enables the teacher to develop techniques suitable and appealing to a general population. An understanding of varying temperaments is the first step to becoming accepting of the differences, but more importantly, that understanding removes some of the frustration teachers often experience when they cannot seem to get a point across after several attempts. One of the best ways to avoid wasted time in the classroom is to present the material so that it appeals to various learning styles and personality temperaments. The majority of the students will grasp the concept being presented much more quickly.

Most of us probably teach in a manner that is representative of our own learning style, the one that best fits our personality temperament. This style becomes our "comfort zone." When we take the chance of extending into the inclusion of zones not as comfortable to us, we begin to reach more students. There are many ways we can present the same material. Inclusion of varied learning styles greatly increases opportunity for success.

The intent of this book is to provide suggestions for practical applications which will guarantee a higher level of performance. Methods and concepts are introduced to simplify and develop understanding of how any singer can execute very artistic phrasing and increase individual musicianship skills. Insights into learning styles and how personality temperaments determine the best style are discussed. Several suggestions for classroom techniques designed to accommodate the differences in various learning styles are given. The teaching techniques are categorized with corresponding learning styles to show how to approach the vast differences in students within the choral rehearsal.

With a combination of sensitivity to differing personality temperaments and simplicity in the approach to educating the student about the artistry of good musicianship, you are certain to have high standards and high morale in your classroom. With these two ingredients, your goals can become reachable and your possibilities infinite.

CHAPTER I

"Finding Time
for Experimentation "

How do we achieve the highest possible level of performance with our students, whether it be the general music class, the non-select choral ensemble, or the auditioned choir? The responsibility lies solely with the teacher/director. The manner in which everything is articulated has a direct effect on the amount of skill that is developed and implemented by the student. Anything that can be articulated or demonstrated *clearly*, so that it is within the level of understanding and ability of the student, probably will be executed as expected.

But what is expected? Do we have preconceived ideas of what we expect our students to be able to do? What is our idea of good tone quality for the age level of the student? What kind of literature should we expect them to be able to perform? How expressive can we expect them to be? How well should they be able to sight-read? Although we need to have a general idea about answers to these questions, if we have preconceived notions about limitations, we have set our expectations of both ourselves and our students. What if we went into the classroom with the idea of not knowing just how far we can take our students? Every day becomes an exciting adventure, a challenge to see just what may be possible. We begin to think in terms of, "If they can do this, let's see what else they can do."

Our students are only limited by our expectations of them. We are limited only by our expectations of ourselves; therefore, our students are really only limited by what we expect of ourselves as teachers. If we set goals but do not limit the expectation in terms of number of goals to achieve, we have guidelines, plans in mind, some structure, but nothing that will inhibit or limit expectations. We then can feel free to experiment with various teaching techniques. Experimentation allows us to expand our expectations and feel the riches of new accomplishment. A teacher who approaches each year with the idea that the new school year brings with it another opportunity to see what is possible, seldom joins the ranks of those who experience "burn-out" after a number of years in the profession.

What is the most important thing to teach our students about good singing? Where do we place the most emphasis in the daily choral rehearsal? Most of us focus on certain areas of teaching that we feel should either be developed before we can approach other areas or we deem certain skills as being the most important to be developed. Many times we focus on areas that we personally feel provide us with the greatest security. They are the areas where we feel we have the most knowledge or the areas we feel the most secure about demonstrating.

None of us languor in excessive amounts of rehearsal time. There is always that feeling of being rushed to get the next performance ready.

Because we always feel that there never is adequate time for preparation, we tend to only get to the things that are most vital to us. We don't allow ourselves the luxury of experimentation, yet experimentation is our most valuable tool. Only through experimentation can we bring our choirs to a higher level of artistry.

How do we find the time for such experimentation? We all know that experimentation takes much more time than plainly stating the facts. None of us ever feels that we have enough rehearsal time. We have too many performances to prepare, too many contests to get ready for, and too much to teach in one short year. Let's see if we can examine some possibilities that might allow us more time for experimentation.

1. <u>**Good Planning**</u>

   This is the most critical ingredient of successful teaching. Everything in the classroom is dependent largely on this one factor. Thorough and intelligent planning will allow for the most effective use of every minute. Discipline problems will almost be completely alleviated by developing efficient use of time. You as the instructor will have confidence in your presentation of material. By spending time to do thorough score study prior to presenting it to the choir and then making every effort to assure that each rehearsal is conducted in as efficient a manner as possible, there will be time for experimentation. Blocks of time can be inserted into the lesson plans for experimental activities that rely on spontaneity, creativity, and visuality.

2. <u>**Teach Sight- Reading**</u>

   For students and teachers alike, nothing is as mundane as "pounding notes." Nothing takes as much time out of a rehearsal for so little feeling of musical accomplishment as "learning by rote." Giving students good reading skills does more to allow the teacher time for experimentation than any other skill. The many hours spent teaching notes can be put to much more exciting use by using that time to expand musical artistry horizons.

3. <u>**Narrow List of Concepts**</u>

   Since all concepts must be repeated over and over in order for the inexperienced singer to understand their application to the musical score, it becomes necessary to economize and find a few concepts that have the greatest cause and effect response. By focusing on a few concepts, more experimental time is available for expanding and developing an understanding of how those concepts are to be applied to all musical explorations.

4. <u>**Use Gestures Instead of Words**</u>

   One simple gesture can often take the place of several words without stopping the rehearsal. Every time a gesture is substituted for verbal explanation, valuable rehearsal time is gained. Also,the more a gesture is used to illicit a response, the more the student will stay focused. (See Picture 1-1)

<u>Picture 1-1</u>

Here is an example of one of many ways we can discover good breathing and vowel formation through experimentation and gestures.

Experimentation allows us to "play with phrases" and find the most artistic shaping and greatest degree of finesse. It allows us to find ways of getting the best tone quality out of the singers. We begin to discover that good vocal production is directly related to how the musical phrase is executed. Good breath support, or breath energy as this author prefers to think of it, is "created" with good phrasing. Once the coordination of phrasing and breath energy are realized, it is very easy to shape vowels and get beautiful tone quality. (See Pictures 1-2 and 1-3)

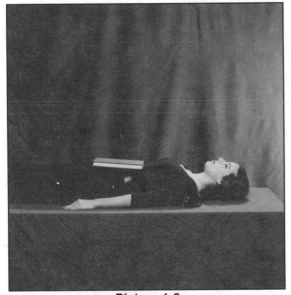

Picture 1-2
Book position during exhalation.

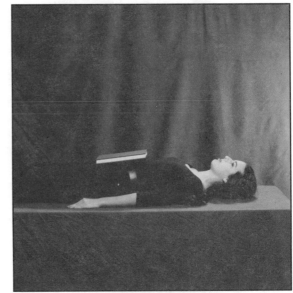

Picture 1-3
Book position during inhalation.

Experimentation is one of the most valuable tools of successful teaching. Teaching can become an exciting game of taking each opportunity that we have to be in the classroom as our chance to "discover" what works more efficiently and achieves higher goals. The more time we have for experimentation, the more exciting it can become. We begin to have time to understand all that is within a musical score. The in-depth study and experimentation of shaping the phrases brings the choir to a much higher level of understanding of the score, which is consequently reflected in the performance. There is nothing as exciting as bringing the choir to a level of artistry that makes the performance an emotional experience long to be remembered by all who took part in it; performer, conductor, and listener.

I'm sure that you can think of many other ways to allow time for experimentation in addition to the above suggestions. Let's take a moment to examine some steps we can take to make those four time-saving devices work for us.

Good Planning

Many teachers are wonderfully creative and come to depend on their intuitive instincts to such a degree that they may forget the value of a well-planned class or rehearsal. Yes, these imaginative, unstructured, free-flowing moments certainly have their place in the classroom. It must be noted that creative skills are invaluable, but the danger exists when the majority of the lesson plans hinge on the ability to "Go where the flow takes you." The lesson "plans" become totally "unplanned" because the teacher relies too heavily on intuitive action.

Many teachers admire those who seem to have such wonderful intuitive powers, but think how those powers might have the opportunity to "blossom" to the fullest extent when good planning has first given a foundation from which to build. Likewise, the very structured teacher needs to draw upon the resources of the intuitive, imaginative teacher. Each type, the intuitive and the structured teacher, can certainly reap great benefits by "borrowing" techniques from the opposite type. We will discuss this at length in the next chapter as we address the implications of differing personality temperaments and learning styles.

Regardless of style, intuitive or structured, moments of exactness and exploration are needed. Good planning allows time for both to exist. Time can be allotted within the lesson plan for moments of exploration. The initial lesson plan need not be adhered to verbatim, but if long range accomplishments are to come to fruition, general arrangements of how we will arrive need be made.

There is nothing as comfortable as walking into the classroom knowing that we have a way to fill every minute and then some, of that class period. Likewise, the longest and most frustrating class periods for most of us, are those where we "plan as we go" and wonder how much longer we have to stretch the time. All of us have been there. Some of us can function very successfully in that manner, but for how long? Most of us walk out of the classroom on a day like that feeling like we were anything but a teacher! We might even ask ourselves, "What am I doing teaching?" We feel a sense of failure that we were destined to from the beginning. How many surgeons do you suppose walk into the operating room not knowing the type of surgery or the specific procedure that will be used? Will they use the procedure that comes to mind as they make the first incision?

Here is one way we might approach a well-planned school year. During the summer preceding a school year, set up a separate folder for each class, (i.e., Mixed Chorus, Girls' Choir, Men's Choir, General Music). As you are spending your summer attending workshops, reading sessions, going to music stores, and looking through a friend's music library, place any piece of music that you think may be appropriate into the designated folder. Also place any sight-reading material that is suitable in the folders. Once you have filled the folders with any materials that might be used for a given class, begin to sort as dictated by your needs. Place music that might be needed for a particular situation in separate stacks. Your stacks might be similar to the following:

1. Christmas or Holiday Concert
2. Contest Selections
3. Selections for the Musical
4. Selections for Community Performances
   (nursing homes, malls, etc.)

5. Spring Concert
6. Selections for Sight-Reading
7. Selections for Learning Experience

The next step is to decide which selections will be introduced in first semester and which in second semester. (We will use the four-quarter, two-semester system as our example.) We will now work with one semester at a time. Count the number of class periods projected for a given class in that semester. If a class meets daily, toss five class periods out for things like announcements, assemblies, unexpected disruptions, etc. If the class meets once a week, toss out two class periods.

Next, take the number of minutes each class period is allotted and allow a certain portion of that time for vocalization and sight-reading. For instance, in a fifty minute period, you might want to allow ten minutes for vocalization (physical and vocal warm-ups as well as developmental vocalization) and another ten minutes for sight-reading. On some days it is also possible to integrate vocalization and/or sight-reading into the music selections chosen for that rehearsal. If your class period is shorter than fifty minutes, you might want to adjust the time allotments accordingly. Be careful not to slight vocalization or sight-reading because you have less time. Make certain to allow for both *every class period* even if time is short. Remember, time invested in these two areas will increase ability to develop other skills.

Using the fifty-minute class period as an example, if we take off the time allocated for vocalization and sight-reading, we are left with thirty minutes per class for all other activities. Let's assume that the number of rehearsals possible in the first semester for a class that meets daily is seventy. Remember, we are going to toss out five rehearsals. Now we multiply the sixty-five rehearsals left by the thirty minutes allocated for each. We have a possible 1950 minutes of rehearsal over 32 hours in the first semester.

We have chosen fifteen pieces we want to study in the first semester. We have already separated the selections into Christmas Concert, educational experience, beginning of the year, and whatever other categories fits our choral program. We must make those decisions to know approximately when we want to begin to work on each piece. Next we separate all music for one semester into levels of easy, moderate, and difficult. We divide our 1950 total minutes of rehearsal time by the fifteen selections. We have approximately 130 minutes per selection. That means we get to work on each selection about eight times for fifteen to twenty minutes. Our next step is to place those eight rehearsals where they function best within our outline for the semester. As we can see, that is not much time, particularly for a difficult piece. In order to compensate for that, we allow the 130 minutes for the moderate selections, half of that (65 minutes) for the easy selections, and double that (260 minutes) for the difficult selections.

This formula allows us to see how little rehearsal time we have for each piece or each activity, as the case may be. We can formulate for a general music class in the same manner by listing activities and music selections for the semester and then following the same formula as was shown for the choral rehearsal. The 130 minutes must include any time spent on discussion of text, composer, phonetic pronunciation of foreign language, rehearsal notes or comments, etc. In other words, we only have 130 minutes total to spend with one of the moderately difficult pieces.

From this we can now place all activities or selections into certain weeks and begin to develop our day-by-day lesson plans. As was previously discussed, we need not conform strictly to following those plans, but we do have a plan. We know where we are headed, we have a good idea of how we are going to get there, and we see how efficiently we must present the material to fit it into a time slot. Consequently, we see how prepared we must be for each class. We realize how important thorough score study is *prior to presenting a piece to the class for the first time.* We must have a pretty good idea of what we expect out of a piece before we begin to teach it. If we are to have time for experimentation with the artistry of the piece, we cannot waste time in the choral rehearsal trying to find out what a few minutes of preparatory score study would have shown us about the piece.

We are now to the point where we can prepare a lesson plan sheet for our students to place in their choir folders. This allows the students to get the music selections in order for the current rehearsal. They also know exactly what our expectations are for them. The fact that we are so well-prepared lets them know that we do not believe in wasting time and they will tend to respect that philosophy more than they would if we appear to come into the class each day seemingly with the "off the cuff" approach. This is not to say that there is no spontaneity in the classroom or some moments of relaxation, but it allows for the students to be aware that those moments only occur at certain times and not commonly throughout every rehearsal.

We will hand out one sheet which shows which pieces will be rehearsed each day and one sheet to show what sight-reading materials will be used. Remember we are going to allow ten minutes for vocalization and at least ten minutes for sight-reading each rehearsal. Any of the techniques or concepts we want to present must be taught and reinforced through the music. Most concepts can be included in the presentation of the sight-reading material and certainly should be reinforced both there and in the vocalization process. For instance, if we present the concept that we do not put extra weight or emphasis on the last syllable of a word, then make certain that as a particular vocalize is being sung, the singer gets accustomed to not putting pressure on the last note of each vocalize. Follow suit in any sight-reading exercise with or without text.

In order to consolidate material and conveniently fit our "lesson plan" onto as few sheets to place in the folders as possible, we will abbreviate titles of pieces and names of books that we will use for sight-reading material. The abbreviations will appear at the top of the lesson plan sheet. **Example 1** below is a sample lesson plan sheet to be placed in each student folder. The plans begin with the second week of school, since the first week was spent with organizational procedures and other necessary beginning of the school year obligations. During the first week, a great deal of time was also spent just getting each class to sing which will be discussed in a later section of this book on motivation and recruitment.

Example 1

Concert Choir - 1st Semester Schedule of Rehearsals

The pieces will be abbreviated in the following manner and you will be asked to get your music in that order each day as you come into rehearsal. This is the first 16 weeks up to your Christmas Concert. Gloria Fanfare - GF , O Come All Ye Faithful - OC , Silent Night - SN, Heilig - H, Baby, What You Going to Be - B, What Is This Fragrance - WF, Joshua - J, School Song - SS, Star-Spangled Banner - SSB, Jeanette Isabella - JI, Go Tell It On the Mountain - GT, O Filii - OF, Loves Antiphon - LA, O Clap Your Hands - CH

Week#/Day – Order of Music			Week#/Day – Order of Music			Week#/Day – Order of Music		
#1	T.	B, WF, SSB, SS	#6	M.	J, CH, LA	#11	M.	SN, H, JI, OC
9/7	W.	LA, SSB	10/12	T.	J, CH, WF, GT	11/16	T.	SN, GF, CH
	T.	H, SS		W.	H, J, CH		W.	H, B, WF, SN
	F.	H, B, WF		T.	CH, J, H, B		T.	OC, CH, H, JI
				F.	CH, J, LA, GT		F.	OF, SN, JI, GT
#2	M.	LA, B, SSB	#7	M.	OF, CH, J	#12	M.	B, GT, OC, GF
9/14	T.	WF, H, LA, SS	10/19	T.	H, OF, CH, LA	11/23	T.	H, JI, SN, CH
	W.	All-Dist. Tryout		W.	OF, CH, WF, H		W.	Review All
	T.	LA, H, SSB		T.	OF, CH, GT			THANKSGIVING
	F.	LA, H, B, WF		F.	B, J, OF, CH			
#3	M.	H, WF, B	#8	M.	GF, OF, CH	#13	M.	J, OF, LA, OC
9/21	T.	LA, H	10/26	T.	J, LA, H	11/30	T.	CH, H, SN, GF
	W.	LA, WF, B		W.	WF, B, GF		W.	OC, H, GT
	T.	H, LA		T.	GF, H, CH, OF		T.	SN, GF, JI, B
	F.	SSB, SS, H, LA		F.	OF, GF, CH, GT		F.	WF, CH, GT
#4	M.	All-Dist. Prep.	#9	M.	Choralier Auds.	#14	M.	SN, GT, OC, WF
9/28	T.	GT, H	11/2	T.	JI, SN	12/7	T.	H, B, CH, JI
	W.	B, GT, H		W.	JI, SN, OC		W.	GF, GT, SN
	T.	WF, GT, H		T.	GF, JI, SN, GT		T.	H, CH, JI, GF
	F.	H, GT		F.	SN, JI, H, OF		F.	WF, B, SN, B, OC
#5	M.	CH, GT	#10	M.	OC, JI, SN	#15	M.	SN, OC, GF, H, GT
10/5	T.	H, CH	11/9	T.	OC, H, GF, SN	12/14	T.	JI, CH, WF, B
	W.	CH, GT, B		W.	SN, OC, GF, H		W.	GT, H, SN, OC
	T.	WF, CH, GT		T.	SN, H, CH		T.	CH, H, JI, GT
	F.	Review All		F.	SN, JI, OC, GT		F.	Discuss Concert

Sunday, Dec. 20 - Decorate for the Christmas Concert. Meet at the auditorium. Time will be specified at a later date. Monday, Dec. 21 - All classes rehearse for the concert during designated hour. CHRISTMAS CONCERT - 7:30pm. Be in seats at 7:00 sharp!

You will receive another sheet with sight-reading instructions for the first 16 weeks. Once any piece is rehearsed three times in class, you could possibly be tested on that piece either individually, in quartets, or in sections. You will only be tested when necessary to determine why progress is not being made as rapidly as it should. If you work in class, you have nothing to worry about!

I'm really looking forward to working with each of you. Please let me know how I can help you. I hope you are half as excited as I am about this year's choir.

Next we develop a similar sheet for sight-reading. Just as the literature must be apropos for the level of the choir, so must the sight-reading material. We must decide what skills we want to instill within the school year, develop a chronological or sequential approach, and choose materials to reinforce the skills. Remember, we have already placed material in the folders for each choir as we were searching for literature. Now we have to decide how that material will fit into our sequential sight-reading presentation. What material is good to introduce new skills, what material serves best as supplemental exercises, and how much preparation must we do before we begin to use any of the material that we have previously filed?

Once we have made these types of decisions, we can place our sight-reading material into different groups. Some of the categories we might want to use in addition to assessing the level of difficulty of each exercise or selection might be as follows:

Scales - Selections that have major scales, chromatic scales, whole-tone scales, and minor scales

Intervals - Selections that introduce material by emphasizing one particular interval and/or selections that utilize intervalic relationships of standard harmony, i.e. triadic movement, do so, d; ti, do, etc.

Pattern groupings -Selections that demonstrate the differences between a sequence, repetition, and mirror; selections that demonstrate differences between polyphonic and homophonic material, etc.

Beginning the Rehearsal

Good planning includes varying the daily routine and being conscious of pacing. Each rehearsal should begin with warm-ups to prepare the singer physically, mentally, and vocally for the rehearsal. For instance, on the day of the Homecoming game and dance, you probably do not need to do vocal or physical exercises designed to energize the singer. Instead, it would be a good time to begin with relaxation exercises and focusing exercises. You might begin by having everyone close their eyes, place all ten fingers of their hands on their thighs, and make sure all ten toes are touching the floor. Now concentrate on sending all tension in the body out the ends of the fingers and toes. There are many similar exercises which promote a calming atmosphere and help to focus on the project at hand. (See Picture 1-4)

Picture 1-4
Beginning the rehearsal with the proper focus is the key to a successful rehearsal.

One of the most difficult tasks on a day like Homecoming or Halloween is to get students to stop talking in order to start class, no matter how much you have worked on the discipline of beginning class on the bell. Once you ask them to close their eyes, as discussed in the exercise above, talk will cease. For some reason there seems to be an unwritten law that the mouth only opens when the eyes are open! Try to find a simple gesture or series of gestures that make certain commands to your students so that you can avoid trying to talk above your students on one of these high excitement days to get the class started. If you have to shout, it sets a tone in the room that is not particularly desirable. It also puts you in the wrong frame of mind. Try something like slowly moving the index finger from one corner of the mouth to the other to indicate "zipping the mouth shut" (silence). Next, with an exaggerated gesture, with both index finger's, point to your eyes as you close them, indicating both silence and closed eyes. Now you can begin to explain what you want them to do. If your students become accustomed to beginning rehearsals with gestures, they will begin to look for them and respond to them. It is all a matter of finding appropriate signals and insisting that your students respond to those signals. We will talk at a later time about the "silent rehearsal," a rehearsal where the conductor does not say a word the entire time. Everything is conveyed through gestures or other means of communication. (See Picture 1-5)

Picture 1-5
*The simple "gesture" of a moving finger is just
one example of substituting gestures for words.*

Once we have done relaxation exercises, we probably want to follow with volcalizes that are fairly slow, rather than fast and peppy. Now that we have established a calm environment and some sense of focus amidst the chaos of their youthful exuberance, we can direct all of the energy that they have into the rehearsal. We can turn what easily could be a wasted rehearsal into a very productive one. In fact, this very likely could become one of the best rehearsals we ever have because of the natural energy created by the excitement of Homecoming.

Most rehearsals call for the opposite approach. Although students display a youthful exuberance prior to the beginning of class, directing that energy into the rehearsal is usually a challenge. One way we can instantly bring energy into the rehearsal is by beginning with a very quick, peppy vocalize such as the one illustrated below in **Example 2**.

Example 2

Zoo-pah, Zoo-pah, Zoo-pah, Zoo-pah,   Zoo.

Continue singing the vocalize in various keys. In order to keep the singer from psychologically tightening as we approach upper registers, move the exercise up a minor third and then down a full step, i. e. from the key of D up to F and then down to E-flat for the above exercise. Sung at a quick tempo, this exercise can promote energy. Using gestures with it will often create even more energy. For instance, ask the students to "stir" the notes as if scooping them off of a table with their hand to keep them moving.   This will create a forward motion of the notes that will cause the vocalize to become a complete phrase rather than each group of two eighth notes being sounded as a separate entity. In order to have the final whole note sung full value with energy, the singers should not only "scoop it off of the table," but also "gradually lift it from the table outward to the middle of the room." (See Pictures 1-6, 1-7, 1-8, and 1-9)

Picture 1-6

The student should become accustomed to using gestures in the rehearsal.

Picture 1-7

Picture 1-8

The gesture must use the entire body.

Picture 1-9

The student can begin to "feel" the musical phrase by using gestures such as this one.

Imagery can play a very important role in presenting concepts to your students. A large portion of this book will deal with the fact that different individuals have different ways of understanding things. Certain types of personalities function very well with a learning style that uses a great deal of imagery, other styles function better with straight facts. We will examine ways to approach all of the various styles, but no matter what learning style we choose to address, no matter how we choose to begin a rehearsal, the one ingredient that must be present in the classroom is a good work ethic.

It is a matter of discipline. Students must be taught the discipline of directing their "playful" energy into "working" energy. There are many ways we can direct energy. Some specific examples will be given in chapter 3. Everything that we approach with our students is dependent on the type of work ethics we have established. Work ethics must be taught. The students must be taught how to concentrate on their singing, what to think about as they are singing, what to listen for in the music, what to strive for in terms of good technique. They must realize that good singing can only occur when both mental and physical effort combine in a strong and consistent work ethic.

Establishing a good work ethic takes patience and persistence on the part of the teacher. It will not be developed rapidly, nor will it remain intact without daily reminders from the teacher. It is so easy to think that things are "set" once we have established a certain routine. The students immediately perceive their opportunity to become a little lackadaisical if we do not reinforce expectations *daily*. All of this takes tremendous energy on the part of the teacher. In order to establish a good work ethic among our students, we as teachers must be prepared to expend a great deal of energy displaying our own willingness to work hard. I recall Robert Shaw's mother making a statement to the effect that her son was not a genius, but that he just knew how to work harder than most people. Most of us probably feel that it is a combination of genius and hard work in his case.

During a conversation recently at a state music convention, one teacher observed how many colleagues had made career changes since the same convention the previous year. The number who had left the field was astonishing. The reasons were varied. The observation left many of us feeling a bit sad and somewhat uneasy.

We all are aware of many reasons talented professionals seek other careers, but all of these conjectures lead us back to one conclusion. There are thousands of extremely talented professionals out there, but the ones who are the most successful are usually the ones who commit themselves to fighting for the things they believe are for the betterment of their program, studying *every single day* to find a way to be more effective in the classroom, taking the time to do the necessary planning for successful teaching in each class period, spending the long hours of going through stacks of music to find what best suits each class, and disciplining themselves to have the energy that it takes to constantly insist with their students that a good work ethic be present in the classroom. In other words, are we willing to run around all the obstacles placed in our path to reach our goal? Any career we choose will have obstacles. There are just different sets for different careers. Whatever we choose, we must be willing to commit to finding a way around the obstacles rather than using them as an excuse to give into less than we know is possible.

Teaching Sight-Reading

Who are the best sight-readers in your choral program? Most of us would probably respond by saying, "Keyboard players." Stop and think about why that might be. What do they study? They certainly have a thorough background in scales because performance of scales is so crucial to developing good keyboard technique. Because they have to be able to read both clefs at once, they must have the ability to determine what interval or triad is on the staff with one quick glance. They also must be able to recognize patterns or groupings at a glance, not to mention that the proficient keyboard player always reads ahead. Are these not the skills that we hope to instill in our singers? If they are, then why shouldn't we teach sight-reading from the standpoint of the keyboard? Once again we are using visuals and imagery that will aid many of our students.

Some small keyboards are rather inexpensive. The students can perhaps provide the batteries required to power them. One need not have keyboards for every student in class. If, for example, there are enough keyboards for one-third of the class, divide the class into thirds by counting off in threes. During the sight-reading exercises begin with the "Ones" reading the notation and playing it on the keyboard. At the same time, the "Twos" can read and sing with solfege (using hand signals) and the "Threes" can read and sing with numbers or with text. Beware of staying with syllables or numbers too long or too often. Most students need to begin using text rather early or the transfer of reading the musical score with text does not develop. Not enough can be said about the advantages of teaching with keyboards. What a great motivational tool!

Remember, the young people today are very accustomed to using visuals. They are computer-oriented. They are used to having "tools" at their disposal. Whether or not we agree that they should be allowed to use "tools" in the learning process, it is the age of technology into which they were born. In order to get them interested in our classes, we have to begin where we can get their interest piqued.

As we begin to teach scales and intervals, the distances and relationships make sense if the student has the keyboard for reference. How many students who play piano do you see "playing" an imaginary piano on their knee as they are sight-reading an example? How many times have you done that yourself? Most of us are very visual creatures. If we stop and think about it, linear measurement would make no sense to us without the use of a rule or yardstick. Maybe the piano keyboard makes that same kind of clarification.

Scales

Not only must the singer understand how scales are constructed, but he must understand how each scale functions within the musical score. We often get into the habit of teaching the Major scale by beginning on the tonic and having the student sing from Do to Do diatonically. How many times in a musical score, whether it be solo literature or four-part choral literature, does the individual choral line employ the use of an entire Major scale? Usually a fraction of the scale is used and often beginning on something other than the tonic. This tells us something about teaching a Major scale to our young singers.

Once the construction of the Major scale is understood, then our singers need to be able to recognize any fragment of that scale in a piece of music. One way we can get them accustomed to searching for those fragments is by working the scale each day from several different directions. Instead of beginning on Do every time we sing the scale, try beginning on Mi. Sing from Mi diatonically ascending to upper Do, drop the octave and sing lower Do diatonically back to where you began on Mi. Then try beginning on La, sing diatonically descending to lower Do, jump the octave up to upper Do and get a sense of finality by singing descending diatonically to So.   See **Examples 2A and 2B.**

Example 2A

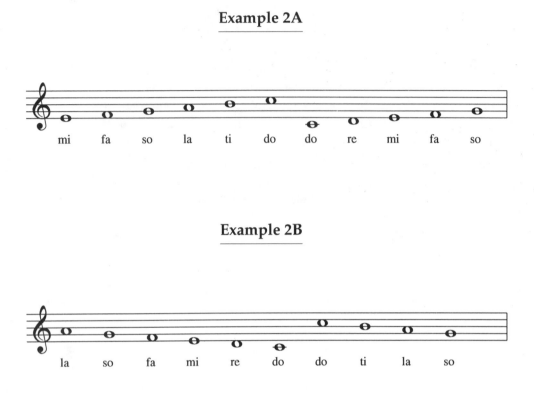

mi   fa   so   la   ti   do   do   re   mi   fa   so

Example 2B

la   so   fa   mi   re   do   do   ti   la   so

Obviously, the singer must understand the placement within the Major scale of the whole and half-steps and how it "feels" and sounds to sing a whole-step and half-step. This takes the training of distinguishing between whole and half-steps up another level. The recognition of the Major scale or any fragment of it will occur *only* when the singer has had the experience of seeing it notated, preferably within the context of a musical score. This transfer is crucial if sight-reading skills are to be developed. Simply teaching the scale by rote-singing will accomplish only a small fraction of the skill needed for good reading, if anything at all. All exercises must be related to musical notation in order for them to serve the singer well.

Example 3 below is a chart that might be kept in a choir folder for reference.

Example 3 — KEYBOARD

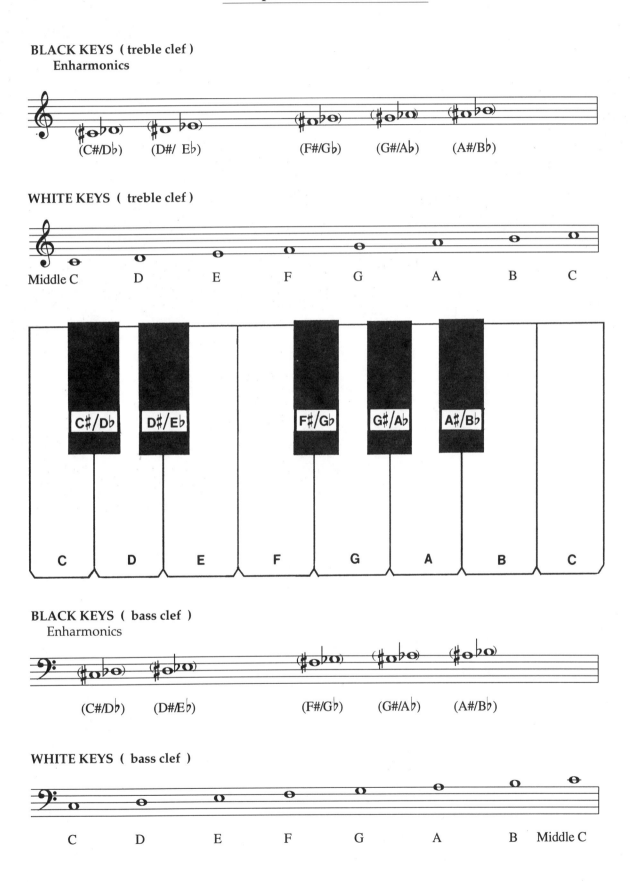

Once the students have a thorough understanding of how the major scale is constructed, it is important to include other scales. If a student can recognize and sing chromatic, whole-tone, minor, and scales in thirds plus the major scales, that student will be a strong sight-reader. We might want to begin by teaching the chromatic and whole-tone scales with words rather than syllables. This author prefers to use the words that Dr. Charlene Archibeque uses with her students at San Jose State University. (Example 4)

Example 4

(Chromatic Scale)

(Use the same text for the descending chromatic scale, bumble bee, bumble bee, bumble, bumble bee.)

(Whole-tone Scale)

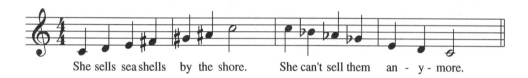

Once the students have become proficient with these words, a transfer over to syllables can be made.

(Scale in thirds) The same words can be used as for the chromatic scale to learn this scale, and again transfer to syllables once the student is secure with the scale.

(Use the same text for the descending scale in thirds.)

Again, the students can transfer to syllables once proficiency has been attained with the words "bumble bee." In order to teach the minor scales, simply choose any major scale and sing from its relative minor by beginning on La below the tonic. **Example 5** shows the C Major scale with its relative minor.

Example 5

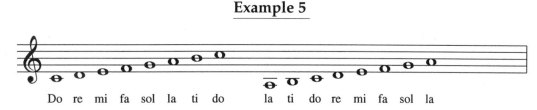

Do re mi fa sol la ti do   la ti do re mi fa sol la

Once the students have become secure with performing these scales, they can be used for intonation exercises in various ways. These exercises will not only develop good intonation, but the students will begin to recognize whole and half-step movement within the musical score with more frequency. Tuning will become automatic and the student will sing descending lines without flatting if proper vocal production is employed. Often, intonation problems have more to do with vocal production than with hearing the intervals, but the student first must know how the intervals sound. Since many students have difficulty hearing chromatics, these exercises are advantageous.

Students are usually familiar with the Major Scale, so it is a good place to begin. Instruct your choir to sing a major scale in unison with every whole-step being sung as a quarter note and each half-step being sung as an eighth-note. See **Example 6**.

Example 6

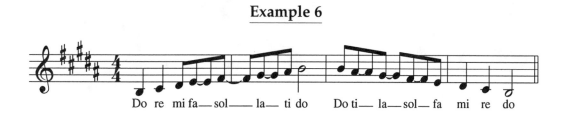

Do re mi fa—sol—— la— ti do   Do ti— la—sol— fa mi re do

The key of B Major seems to fit most voices comfortably for all of the above scales.

Once the students are comfortable with this rendition of the major scale, divide them into two groups. Group I will sing the major scale as indicated in Ex. 6 , Group II will sing the chromatic scale with eighth-notes. The idea is to tune each whole and half-step of the major scale, which is more familiar to them, to all of the half-steps in the chromatic scale. To develop individual skills, pair off in twos; with students facing each other, one sings the major scale while the other sings the chromatic scale in the same manner that the two groups did. See the diagram in **Example 6A** to see how the two scales will sound together ascending and descending.

Example 6A

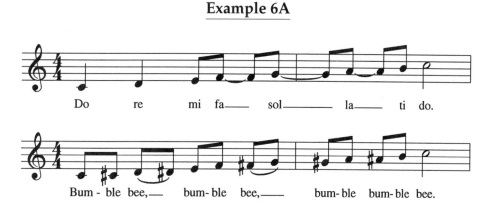

Do   re   mi fa——   sol———— la—— ti do.

Bum - ble bee,——   bum- ble bee,———   bum-ble bum- ble bee.

Another exercise combines the whole-tone scale with the chromatic scale. The whole-tone scale would be sung in quarter notes, the chromatic scale in eighth notes. Using these exercises as part of the choral warm-up rapidly increases skills of both reading and singing in tune. Not enough can be said about the value of incorporating this into a daily routine, especially if it is related to the piano keyboard and the musical score. Draw a picture of a piano keyboard on the blackboard with a staff below it indicating how the pitches of the keyboard would look in music notation. (The diagram should be similar to the one on page 15.) As the chromatic scale is being introduced to the singers for the first time, point to the keys of the keyboard that correspond to the pitches that are being sung. The students should "play" on their imaginary keyboards, by giving each one a diagram like the one you have put on the board to keep in their choir folders. Better yet, use small battery-operated keyboards in the classroom.

The students begin now to understand the "size" and "sound" of a half-step. (A diagram is illustrated below for placement in the choral folders.)

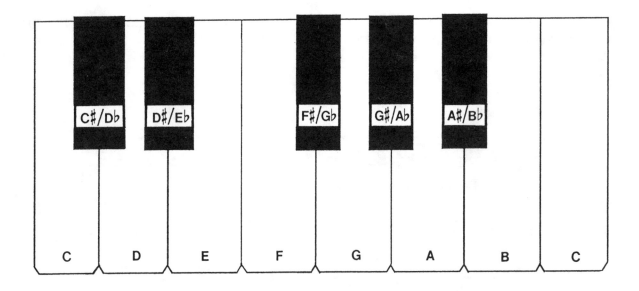

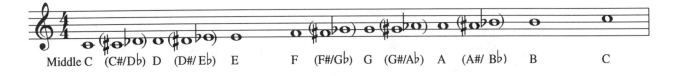

Middle C (C#/Db) D (D#/Eb) E   F (F#/Gb) G (G#/Ab) A (A#/Bb) B   C

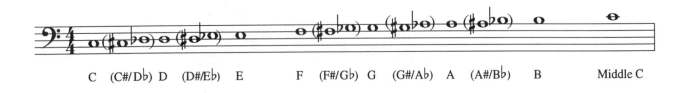

C (C#/Db) D (D#/Eb) E   F (F#/Gb) G (G#/Ab) A (A#/Bb) B   Middle C

Next, ask the students to look at the blackboard and focus only on the staff. Sing the chromatic scale again as you point to the pitches on the staff. Finally, make them search for fragments of a chromatic scale within the musical score such as it appears in the King's Singers arrangement of Henry Leslie's, "Charm Me Asleep." (Hinshaw #HMC-827) example. Only treble voicings of the SSATBB arrangement are shown to demonstrate our point, although many examples of chromatics can be found throughout the entire piece. This is a beautiful piece of music that certainly demands that the singer exercise and develop good ear-training skills as well as good musicianship.

CHARM ME ASLEEP

Music by HENRY LESLIE
Arranged by the King's Singers

As you can see from the example, there is the added task of one voice part picking up where another left off in order to continue the chromatic scale. To help tune and develop linear flow from one voice part to another, have a few of your best singers in each section sing two or three notes of the entrance that takes over, and then drop out. (i. e., a few altos would sing the first few notes of the second soprano entrance in measure 44 before dropping out as the score indicates) Don't forget to include sight-reading material that uses chromatic movement, such as church hymns.

Intervals

Next, the students must have a thorough knowledge of intervalic and chordal relationships. They must *know* how the intervals look on the staff in relation to how they <u>sound</u>. This is where the piano keyboard proves to be such an asset. We can simplify by grouping the intervals within a major scale into two groups   the even intervals which are always line to space or vs., and the odd intervals which are always line to line, or space to space. The even intervals, 2nd, 4th, 6th, and octave, are line to space (or vs.) with no line, one line, two lines, or three lines in between, consecutively. The odd intervals, prime, 3rd, 5th, and 7th, are the same note or line to line or space to space with no lines or spaces between, one line or space between, or two lines or spaces between, consecutively. See Example 7.

Example 7

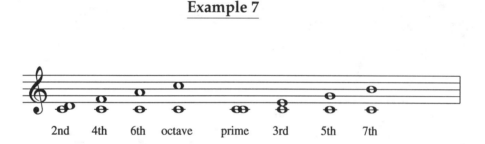

2nd - line to space

4th - line to space, one line between

6th - line to space, two lines between

octave - line to space, three lines between

prime - same note

3rd - line to line

5th - line to line, one line between

7th - line to line, two lines between

Rhythm

Let's look at a way to present rhythm. I found when I taught junior high school for so many years that many of my younger students did not have a good grasp of the concept of fractions. In order to compensate for this, I started teaching rhythm from the standpoint of the eighth-note being introduced first. Everything else was then related proportionately to the eighth-note. I also discovered that my students understood multiplication much better than division. This prompted me to use the following method to introduce rhythmic concepts.

First, everything in the beginning is introduced with whole numbers (we do not talk about an eighth-note equaling one-half of a count.) Next, every time we take something away from the note, that note doubles in value. We will begin by assuming that an eighth-note is one count. If we remove the flag from the eighth-note, it becomes a quarter note and is held for two counts. If we remove the coloring from the note head, the quarter note becomes a half note and is held for four counts. If we remove the stem from the half-note, it becomes a whole note and is held for eight counts.

I now suggest putting a chart on the board or handing out a worksheet to reinforce this idea of proportion. On the chart, change the number of counts that an eighth-note equals to various amounts and by the rule of proportion, figure what the doubled amounts would be. Next assign one-half and one-fourth counts to the eighth note and instruct the students to apply the rules of proportion to the other notes. Finally, use the following chart to reinforce the rules of proportion. See **Example 8**.

Example 8

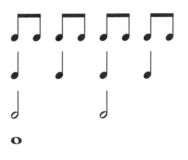

Now we are ready to introduce the rule of the dot. *The dot always get one-half of whatever is in front of it.* Finally, we introduce the sixteenth-note and its various combinations. All of this can be introduced through the use of ties.

We can introduce a method of counting along with the presentation of all of the above material.

By using this method of proportion, time signatures do not become confusing. When rhythm is introduced with the quarter note getting one count in $\frac{4}{4}$ or common time switching to $\frac{6}{8}$ causes nothing but confusion, let alone cut time or other time signatures.

Once we have introduced the rules of proportion, we can then say that the only proportions we will commonly use are those where the eighth-note equals one-fourth, one-half, or one count. We soon discover that the bottom note of the time signature tells use three things: the kind of note that gets one count, the number of the note that gets one count that are contained in the whole note (this is important if we are to keep reinforcing rules of proportion), and the number of counts that the whole note gets in that particular time signature. For instance, in $\frac{6}{8}$ time: the eighth-note gets one count, there are eight eighth-notes in a whole note, and in this time signature, the whole note gets eight counts.

Playing the keyboard will enhance rhythmic articulation more than just clapping rhythms, because the rhythmic attack and release must be prepared and thought about in advance. *Singing is a series of preparations!*

We must always remember that whether we are sight-reading or preparing a score for performance, we must prepare by looking ahead, so our students must be taught to look ahead as they are learning to sight-read. As mentioned, the use of keyboards in the classroom is one way to approach this, since the attack and release of the key must be prepared and thought about in advance. Students must also become aware of repetition, sequences, and mirrors. They must learn to look for patterns, both melodic and rhythmic. Where is the melodic material a fraction of a scale, any of the scales we have studied? Where does sequential material appear? Where do major skips occur? I teach my students to look at melodic lines in the following manner:

( ) = same pitch

$\overset{3}{\vee}$ = skip (the size of the interval indicated with a number 3 for a third, etc.)

╱ or ╲ = scalewise (diatonic movement). If the scale is anything other than major, indicate with the letter C for chromatic and the letter W for whole-tone. Minor forms shall be indicated with m-h (minor-harmonic form) m-m (minor-melodic form) and just m for the natural minor

$\overset{S}{[\ ]}\ \overset{R}{[\ ]}$ = pattern (above the pattern S= sequence, R= repetition, and M= mirror.)

Example 9

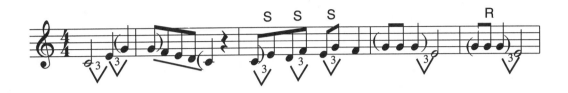

Here is another activity we can use to sharpen reading skills. Write a melody line on the board, **Example 9**, and instruct your students to begin singing the melody using syllables. Periodically as they sing the example, snap your fingers indicating that they are then to switch to numbers, back to syllables, etc. You could snap from three to five different times in the above example. Vary by having them sing backwards from the last measure.

Next, write a simple melodic line on the board and sing it using syllables or numbers. Then challenge them a bit more by saying the first pitch of the line is now the fifth of the scale rather than the tonic. The above example would be sung with the key signature of F Major now, rather than C Major. Next, assign the first note as the fourth of the scale. The new key would be G Major, but the students should first identify where to place half and whole-steps, then sing it, finally, figure out the key.

These are just a few exercises that I use to teach sight-reading skills. There could be another whole book written just on sight-reading technique. There are many good ones on the market. The key to making your students successful is not necessarily the method, but the consistency with which you present the material and the frequency with which you have your students practice sight-reading. Remember you MUST teach sight-reading if you are to have time to teach your students to enjoy the artistry of making music!

The other two time-saving devices mentioned at the beginning of this chapter (narrowing the list of concepts and using gestures instead of words) will be discussed throughout this book and will not appear in separate headings. One example of narrowing the list of concepts was given in the rules of proportion for introducing rhythm. It certainly saves time to show the proportion rule rather than teach one time signature at a time. Many of the concepts will be presented throughout the book that this author feels are time-saving. The gestures will be discussed as we begin to talk about imagery and how it elicits responses from the singer.

Before we can begin to talk about concepts, gestures, etc., we must understand that we deal with the general population in our classroom. Our students understand concepts in differing ways. In order for us to make as many of our students feel successful as possible, we must find ways to teach that satisfy these different styles of learning. We will come closer to making this possible if we have an understanding of the differences, can come to appreciate those differences, learn to use the differences as an advantage to broaden both our knowledge and the knowledge of our students, understand our own learning styles and personality temperaments, and finally develop a teaching technique that includes the different styles.

This page left intentionally blank.

CHAPTER 2

"Learning Styles and Their Indications"

What type of teacher do you prefer, the one who gets straight to the point and presents the facts or the one who uses analogies? Do you have a clearer understanding of a concept when the end result is shown first and the steps which lead to the result are then presented or do you more easily grasp the essence by taking one step at a time and leaving the result to be discovered as an outgrowth of working those individual steps? Which do you enjoy more, working with concrete facts and figures, or drawing upon your imaginative and creative skills? Do you need to see something in the written word in order to remember it, or does just hearing it usually suffice? Do you relate as easily to something that is presented with imagery as something which is presented visually? Are you more of a visual learner or more of an auditory learner? The way you respond to these questions is a strong indication of the learning style with which you feel the most comfortable.

In the classroom, most of us are going to teach in a manner compatible with our own learning style because of the security that allows us. We tend to think that because we understand a concept best if presented in a certain manner, so will our students. The most frustrating part of teaching is having to say something over and over only to have our students say that they still do not understand. As more time is wasted by repeating ourselves, frustrations build with both the student and the teacher and eventually both give up. We seek justification as a teacher by saying to ourselves, "That concept is still too complex for them. They need to be more mature before I can expect them to grasp it." We might even say, "Oh well, maybe it's not so important for them to understand that particular concept."

We have often said as teachers that we must be able to say the same thing a "million different ways." We may choose a few different words, but we really don't take new approaches. With knowledge of various learning styles and understanding the implications of each, we can find suitable approaches to the material we want to present. In fact, we no longer need to find a "million ways" to say the same thing, but often can be successful with two diverse ways. Only if we have a clear picture of the diversity with which individuals perceive things can we begin to find methods to accommodate those differences. To gain an idea of how broad the spectrum is, ask one of your classes to describe any simple object, such as a chalkboard eraser. Hold up the eraser and ask, "How would you describe this?" You will be amazed at some of the answers, particularly the ones contrary to your own description. You probably will consider some of the answers either dull, boring, unimaginative or bizarre and totally unrelated, depending on your own perceptions and learning style.

Picture 2-1

Different attitudes of the sensing vs. intuitive learning styles.

In order to understand learning styles, we have to deal with more than whether an individual is "right-brained" or "left-brained." (See Picture 2-1) According to Kiersey and Bates (1978), the entire **personality temperament** is a determinant. In their book, "Please Understand Me," the sixteen different combinations which form to categorize specific personality types are clearly outlined. Much of the information in this chapter is derived from combining a study of that book with this author's own observations and experiences from more than twenty-five years of teaching.

Once an understanding is gained about various combinations of the four areas which form our **personality temperament**, it is easier to appreciate the differences and consequently remove some of the misunderstandings about why some teaching techniques are not as successful as we would hope they might be. In turn, that allows us to develop techniques which are more suitable to what we have in the classroom. Appreciation of the differences makes us more sensitive to those who appear to be our "opposites" instead of being impatient and critical because they do not "see" things the same as we do. We can draw upon the resources made available to us by the differing personalities through use of cooperative learning activities.

Kiersey and Bates (1978) talk about preferences and how those preferences are paired with other preferences to determine personality temperament, hence learning styles. They suggest that each of us is born with certain tendencies; our experiences either strengthen those tendencies or allow them to become less dominant. The preferences are placed into four categories. Let's begin with a study of those four categories of preferences.

Introversion vs. Extroversion

This quality of a particular personality temperament is the one that is most apparent to the outside observer. Observe your students as they enter the classroom, especially the first day of school. Which students come into the room interacting with several different people, which are basically speaking to one other person or not speaking to anyone at all? Where do they choose to sit, in the middle of a group or more to the outer fringes?

Are you more introverted or more extroverted? Which is your natural preference? How do you think teaching has altered your natural preference? These questions are asked because many of the decisions you make about discipline and how you evaluate your students *could* depend on your personal preferences toward introversion and extroversion.

Because we are in the performing arts, we often consider extroversion to be synonymous with confidence, and encourage this to ensure better performances from our students. However, we discourage that same form of "confidence" when it comes to discipline in the classroom. We are sending mixed signals. The social skills of the extrovert tend to become our "discipline problems" because of their constant need for interaction with others, their desire to socialize and be popular.

The extrovert does not mind sharing a folder with someone, doing group projects (cooperative learning), or eating lunch with a large group, even though many may be strangers to him. The introvert usually prefers to have his own folder or share with one other close friend. He prefers working alone or with one other person he feels he can trust. The introvert prefers to have lunch in a more quiet area and often with just one friend.

I recall a high school senior requesting to eat during her usual lunch period when the schedule for that day dictated that we change lunch periods. Her comment was that she knew no one in the other lunch period and she preferred skipping lunch to eating in the lunchroom during a lunch period that was not her routine schedule. Considering one-third of the school eats during any given lunch period, there was more than a good chance of her finding someone in the lunchroom that she knew, but she was not willing to take that risk. This student is in one of my women's choruses and in many ways exhibits classic behavior of an introvert. She wants to sit in the back of the room, she is very hesitant to "sing out." I have also noticed that she rarely speaks to anyone before class other than the one girl with whom she shares a folder. Unlike this particular young lady, the extrovert can't wait to see who else might be in the lunchroom. The change of routine and the new social contact energizes the extrovert.

Observe your students. What students become actively involved in the class activities, which do not? The introvert can seem as if he is a slow learner because he holds back, thinks quietly to himself and often is self-doubting. He is frequently misunderstood.

According to Kiersey and Bates the desired attitude will have more potency, although we are all predisposed to some qualities of each personality temperament. Extroverts are energized by other people, introverts are energized from within. Introverts prefer private space where solitary activities take place such as reading, sewing, fishing, etc. Socialization stimulates and energizes the extrovert. Rarely will an extrovert seek solitude. Extroverts tend to want to be involved in group activities; sports, music groups, parties, etc. The extrovert usually wants to study for exams with someone while the introvert prefers to study alone.

Knowing what type of student we have in the classroom will help us make decisions about our approach to teaching. Obviously, discipline is strongly influenced by the number of extroverts we have in the classroom and where we place them in relation to each other. Another consideration we need to make is how well will the introvert perform in a situation where he is totally surrounded by extroverts. If we group all of the extroverts together, we will definitely have to work harder at getting their attention. A good mixture is best if we do not put one introvert in among several extroverts. However, if extroversion includes 75% of the population as indicated by Bradway and Myers (1964), it will be very difficult to get a good distribution.

To understand which students have qualities of extroversion and which have qualities of introversion in your classroom, try the following exercise, tell your students to get into groups of ten or more. Tell them to choose one person to take notes and be able to repeat the decisions of the group. The group does not have to agree on any of the decisions. All suggestions should be listed by the person selected to record the discussion. The group project is to decide what would be an ideal weekend.

Observe and listen to the discussions among each of the groups. A certain pattern will emerge. You will begin to see which students prefer quiet time alone or with very few people and which prefer a lot of activity centered around situations involving several people. Once you have been able to outline the distinctions of the opposing ideas, reassign the students to the group that most appeals to them and continue the discussion for a few more minutes. When you have placed them into the group that best suits their individual choices, you will be able to observe very distinct differences. The group that prefers a lot of activity will be very loud in their continued discussion, partially because they will all want to talk at once, making certain that they have their say. There will be great desire to be included in the group and interaction with as many people as possible. The group that prefers more solitude will be very quiet and automatically take turns, one at a time expressing their thoughts.

Once we have an idea of which of our students are extroverts and which are introverts, we must consider in a choral ensemble how not only discipline but performance quality will be affected by placement of personnel. Is the introvert the most timid singer? If we surround light lyric voices with heavier voices, will the singer with the lighter quality put undo strain on the vocal mechanism by trying to keep up with the surrounding instruments? Can we get more projection from the timid singer by surrounding him with stronger examples? To answer all of these questions we need to ask, "What is the most healthy for all singers? This question can only be answered through experimentation with your singers to see which way seems to produce the best results for all concerned. It might mean that you place your singers one way for rehearsal and another way for performance.

You may want your rehearsal set up so that one singer can learn from another but not be dependent on each other during a performance. What if you begin to work with your choir so that a good mixture of introverts and extroverts are placed strategically within sections. You may want the timid singer placed close to someone who is not so timid, (not necessarily synonymous with introversion/extroversion). The singer who is timid may be very extroverted but not secure with his voice as a musical instrument. In a performance, all singers need to be placed where the people surrounding them help make each other's voices sound as beautiful as possible. You certainly would not want to place two singers one in front of the other if they both sing with a strident tone. It will only bring out those undesirable qualities. *Remember, the singer hears the sounds from behind more than those beside him in choral riser formation.*

Experiment with your singers to see which way produces the best result. Try placing like voice qualities vertically rather than horizontally in the choir formation. Place more lyric voices to the back of the risers or room so that they don't hear heavier voices from behind them. If they try to emulate the heavier voice quality, it will only cause forced and manipulated tone.

Place the best blending voices in the center of the choir since that is the sound you want to be dominant. Sound carries stronger from the center of the choir. Place your voices with more of a solo quality to the outer edges. Often, when the solo quality type of voice is placed to the outer fringes, the singer feels a little more alone and will back off some to hear the other voices. Consequently, he will begin to blend a little better with the rest of the choir. If you place a solo voice near too many other heavy voices, it only encourages him to try and compete, so again it is probably wise to place the more lyric voices to the top of the riser. Have you ever noticed that when students are selected for an all-district choir, one of the major problems when they first start to rehearse is that they all compete vocally with one another? All of a sudden they are surrounded by voices as strong and stronger than their own and they feel the urge to compete. If they are not made aware that this is what is happening, they will all end up "donating their vocal chords to medical science." It is not so unlike that in the pecking order within your own choir, so placement of individuals and voices must be a consideration for the well-being of vocal health. Time needs to be allowed for listening within sections as well as quartets of mixed voicing. This author prefers to perform with a choir formation of mixed voicing. Not only does this teach the singer to be independent, he can hear the musical score and blend with a better sense of ensemble. It is a little unreasonable to expect our singers to blend with an ensemble if they cannot hear an ensemble sound.

To summarize the findings of Kiersey and Bates, extroverts are renewed by contact with other people. They feel lonely when not around others. Introverts feel lonely and uncomfortable in crowds. Introverts go through life feeling that they ought to be more sociable, perhaps because 75% of the population leans more toward extroversion. (Bradway, 1964) They enjoy others but it is a drain on their energy to be around a lot of people. Extroverts are drained of their energy if they do not have others to re-charge their batteries. Under duress, the opposite will surface. You will see the extrovert become very private and vice versa. There is some indication that the reason opposites may attract is because we admire those qualities in others that we do not seem to have.

Our first order of business, whether we are dealing with introverts or extroverts, is to make our students feel successful by building their confidence. This is a slow process. We begin by setting them up for success, making certain that what we ask them to do is not only possible but something they can do with confidence. It may be as simple as asking them to tell their name to the class, although even this may be difficult for the introvert or the timid extrovert. The first day of school is a great opportunity to begin setting up a positive attitude in your students. Most of us explain class rules, telling students everything they cannot do, hand out textbooks, and give homework assignments. We will call roll, mispronouncing names and set ourselves up to lose the class. By having your students tell their own names, what choral experience they have had in the past, and what part they most recently sang, you get several things accomplished. Since these are questions they know the answers to, no one is put on the spot. As they say their names, check them off the roster, make notes of pronunciation and whether Richard would rather be called Rich, Rick, Dick, or Richard. Make assessments about their voices, thick or thin quality, lyric, etc. On the students who have not sung for several years, get an idea from their speaking voices as to which section you might place them in until you have been able to make a more formal assessment of their voices.

Have the students stand in a circle rather than sit at their seats for this exercise. This will discourage conversation among themselves and encourage them to listen to each other, especially if you offer some kind of reward for the student who can remember the most names at the conclusion of the exercise.

You can begin to make observations and have an idea of who the introverts might be by the way they react to the activity. They may be slow to join the circle, searching for the most inconspicuous place within it.

They probably will not converse with others as they head for the circle from their seat. After the exercise, seat the students according to voice parts. It sometimes is wise on the first day to allow them to sit by a person of their choice within the section. This will also allow you to make some important observations.

You are now prepared to sing the first day. What a refreshing change from being given rules, homework, and being told what you cannot do for the rest of the year. Whose class do you suppose they will want to return to the next day?

As far as singing the first day, choose something that will cause them to be successful. One thing that works well for all ages is the canon "Himmel und Erde." So much can be taught from this one simple melody that it is all you need to use to present most basic concepts of good musicianship.

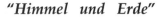

"Himmel und Erde"

You will have to say very little if anything about discipline because you have shown your students what is expected. You probably have also had time to present a couple of pieces of music in addition to the canon and maybe even some rhythmic exercises to begin teaching literacy skills. The idea is to fill that first day so full and pace it so fast that the students understand that there is no time to waste. Each day will be filled with activity and learning. Do not give them time to set themselves up for discipline problems. This way the introvert will feel more comfortable getting involved in the activity because attention is not drawn to specific individuals other than in the introductory circle. The extrovert simply doesn't have the opportunity to socialize but gets involved in the activities because he wants to be with the group.

Sensible vs. Intuitive

Kiersey and Bates describe the second characteristic of one's **personality temperament** as sensation versus intuition. They describe the person who fits the sensation mold as one who says he is practical. He wants facts, reality, and believes in experience. He is interested in others experiences, believes in what is actual and doesn't worry about what might be. He is accurate in his observations because he notices details. The intuitive, on the other hand, describes himself as innovative and creative. He often just scans his surroundings, missing details noted by the sensible because he is only aware of that which relates to his current preoccupation.

The intuitive enjoys fantasy, uses imagery and metaphors. He explores beyond reality, looks for what is possible rather than what is, is attracted to the future, not the past or the actual. Because of this he relies on hunches, which makes him vulnerable in the sense that ignoring reality too long causes him to lose touch with it. He is also subject to greater error than other personality types because of his tendency to make judgements on his intuitions. Complex ideas do come to him, although he is unable to explain how he knew. If asked how he knew or how he arrived at the idea, he is most apt to respond with, "It just came to me one day." Sensible people tend to ignore hunches. Their ability to receive them diminishes as a result.

The intuitive always lives in anticipation and becomes restless and dissatisfied easily. He tends to go from one activity to another without completing any. The sensible values experience and the wisdom of the past and is considered to be very down to earth, no nonsense, and practical. He depends on perspiration, the intuitive depends on inspiration. (Kiersey and Bates, 1978)

There are obvious advantages to each type. This however, is where the greatest gap in the ability for one to understand the other lies. One type often has grave misunderstandings about the other type. Any success in teaching is proportionate to our ability to incorporate both styles into our teaching techniques. It is very difficult however to teach in an intuitive manner if we innately are the sensible type and vice versa. As teachers, we must learn to be sensitive to both temperaments.

One place to start is to be open to learning from our student's. We are bound to have both types in the classroom, although again Bradway and Myers indicate 75% the population to be sensible and 25%, intuitive. One of the best ways to get a student to remember a concept is to have him teach it. By involving students in the teaching process, we reap the benefits of seeing how they would present a concept based on their own learning style. We can ask a student whom we know to be of the opposite temperament from our own, how he sees a certain concept. *As teachers, our best chance for success is if we remain students ourselves for the rest of our lives*. Although this includes continuing formal education, it also includes trying to learn something new in our classrooms every single day.

To determine what the personality temperament of your students might be, look for daydreamers, students who seem to like fantasy, students who seem uninvolved, inattentive, opinionated, and you will have a good indication that they are intuitive. Wouldn't it be interesting to see what percentage of A.D.D. (Attention Deficit Disorder) students also are intuitive? The intuitive student will also be passionately devoted to his friends. Because he may have the tendency to form inappropriate crushes, it is wise for you, as his teacher, to be careful to keep a good balance in the rapport that you develop with this type of student. One thing that will destroy the confidence that he has in you is breaking a promise. Make certain that you can follow through with statements that you make, without regret. Consider any statements you make to an intuitive student to be a promise. (Kiersey and Bates, 1978)

Observation of the sensible student will show that he takes a change of plans in his stride, gives power easily to others, wants things to make sense, responds to detail, and relates to the real world. If the teacher has an awareness of student reactions, many of these qualities will make themselves apparent. Kiersey warns that the intuitive child is more likely to be difficult.

Here is an exercise to partially determine which way your students lean. Use the groups in the same manner as with the previous exercise for extroversion vs. introversion. This time set a piece of chalk, an eraser, a set of keys, or any objects that you wish in the front of the classroom and ask the groups to describe the objects. Some students will ask if you want them described in certain terms such as color, what they are used for, etc. Your response should be, "Do whatever the word describe means to you." With that initial question from your students, they are already demonstrating their individual qualities toward certain learning styles. Some students will come to the front of the room to handle the objects. This is a distinction of the "sensibles" because they use the 5 senses to describe.

Again, you will see group distinctions as previously discussed. The sensible group will describe in terms of color, sound, taste, measurement, usefulness, etc. The intuitive group will relate the objects to something else. Some students will even demonstrate with body language or vocally how absurd they think an answer is. Follow through by regrouping into desired styles and continue discussion for a few more minutes. Give the students a chance to discuss with the group where they feel more comfortable. Remember, we are trying to build confidence. Always go back and let students interact with those whom they feel the most comfortable with because they are of like temperaments or styles.

Thinking vs. Feeling

The third set of qualities that help determine **personality temperament** are thinking versus feeling. The thinking personalities make choices on an impersonal basis, the feeling personalities on a personal basis. Both make choices, but in the way more comfortable to them. The thinkers are most comfortable with impersonal, objective judgments. Feelers value personal judgments. It is all a matter of preference, but misunderstandings occur when one is forced to make judgments in an uncommon way. Formal schooling addresses the thinker, so the feelers develop both sides out of necessity in order to function in the school setting. The feelers are seen as emotionally sensitive. Although both have emotions of the same intensity, feelers are more apt to show theirs. The key is to understand and appreciate the differences because both sides need each other to present another point of view.

According to Kiersey, thinkers latch on to words like justice, categories, standards, criteria, principles, policy, law, etc. Feelers are attracted to words like subjective, values, extenuating circumstances, intimacy, appreciation, sympathy, and devotion. Once again, if we as teachers show a strength toward one side or another, it will determine our reaction toward our students. The thinking teacher will tend to say, "I'm really sorry your dog died last night, but you knew over a week ago that your paper was due today." The feeling teacher would probably extend the deadline. The students know what water cannot be tested with the thinking teacher but will always try to find where the emotional limitations are with the feeling teacher. A feeling teacher often has more difficulty making decisions about what is fair and correct. Once the students realize that there may be some emotional bargaining power, they will use it to the fullest extent. There also may be that one student who is encouraged to go on because of an attitude that a thinking teacher may take with him. Some students stay in class because a teacher takes the time to listen and does show empathy. There must be a balance however between healthy empathy and pity. No student needs a teacher who becomes an enabler and allows him to use pity as an excuse to not learn responsibility.

Every teacher has interaction with a student that they wish they could take back. Sometimes the results of our suggestions are not at all what we had anticipated. We need to draw from the experiences of our colleagues and do our best to help our students. That is all anyone can ask of us. Once we have given the very best we know how to give, we cannot berate ourselves for what might have been. We do well to be in control of ourselves let alone try to be responsible for all of our students. Ultimately, we are there to teach them how to be responsible for themselves. We can only guide them to the best of our ability. Our ability will be at its best when we are willing to listen to and learn from others. One thing students will always recognize in a teacher is honesty.

Kiersey says that one way we can determine whether a child is a thinker or a feeler is to observe him when asked to respond in a situation he does not quite understand. He says to observe whether the child tends to ask for reasons or does the child tend to seek to please? In summarizing qualities of each side Kiersey says to note these descriptions of the thinker: wants reasons to be asked to do something, may not want to be touched, may have difficulty showing affection but hurts inside as much as the feeler. The feeling child wants to know he is pleasing the other person with his obedience, he is willing to perform services for others but needs to be shown appreciation, he is sensitive to emotional climate, and can become physically ill with conflict. One of the most striking differences between the two sides is the will of the feeling person to want harmonious human relationship above all else. He will often concede a point of argument for the sake of that harmony. The thinking person does not feel that sort of conflict and will make great effort to get a point across if he truly believes it with no regard for the resolve that conceding might bring.

Our exercise to determine some differences in the classroom can be done in groups as before with the question posed, "What do you want to be remembered for?" Although most of the answers will be very similar in nature, usually stock answers that have been socially learned, there will be subtle differences. The thinkers usually want to be remembered for having accomplished something with their lives, the feelers are more concerned with being remembered as a passionate person.

Judgmental and Perceptive

The final category by which we determine **personality temperaments** is judgmental vs. perceptive. This category is deceiving by name as it does not mean that a person is judgmental of others or perceptive of other's feelings, although some of the qualities that are indigenous to each side may cause one to become rather judgmental or perceptive. The best way to describe the differences is to say that a judgmental personality prefers things settled, closed, decided; whereas, the perceptive personality prefers the open-ended, tentative, undecided. Judgmental is very task-oriented, perceptive is not.

The judgmental temperament has an urgency pending until decisions are made. Only then is there satisfaction and release of stress. This person takes deadlines very seriously and expects the same from others. This can be a constant source of irritation in relationships. The work ethic of the judgmental individual has a marked effect on what he is willing to do to get the job completed. He is very outcome oriented.

The perceptive temperament resists making decisions wanting more data. He is restless and uneasy with decisions. He holds out and ignores deadlines much to the dismay of the judgmental temperament. For him the work process must be enjoyable. He is less serious. He must allow time for play. He is process-oriented rather than outcome-oriented. He is better able to adapt than his opposite. He is more flexible. Where the judgmental personality will always set aside time first for work, the perceptive personality will first set aside time for play. I recall one of my friends who tested strongly as a perceptive personality making the comment in July that he had yet to file his income tax for the previous year. The judgmental temperament likes things planned-ahead, settled, decided, completed compared to the desires of the perceptive temperament who likes things to be pending, flexible, tentative, and an attitude of "let's wait and see." I quote from Kiersey, "One's temperament is that which places a signature or thumb print on each of one's actions, making it recognizably one's own."

For this exercise, choose a difficult task such as describing the word, "love." Tell the students they have only five minutes to come up with a description. Observations will allow you to recognize that there are those students who come up with three or four words to describe the word and then go on about their business, doing something totally unrelated to the task. These students fit the perceptive temperament. There are others who will use the entire five minutes to keep coming up with more words to describe the word, "love." They feel compelled to keep working on the task for the assigned number of minutes in order to satisfy requirements completely. They will not move on to anything else until the teacher says the time is up. Assigning a time limit and insisting that the task be completed at that time is very upsetting to the perceptive personality. He usually will avoid being put in that position.

Kiersey goes on to show how certain combinations of indicators form predictions of personality temperaments to a greater extent. From this point on, the personality temperaments will be abbreviated by a single letter as follows: E=extrovert, I=introvert, S=sensitive, N=intuitive, T=thinking, F=feeling, J=judgmental, and P=perceptive.

Kiersey describes the **SP (sensitive/perceptive)** as one who must be free, not obligated, to do as and when he wishes. He enjoys today without regard for tomorrow, nothing is saved. He does things not because he has a goal or end result in mind but because he has an urge. He often does things on a whim. He covets the impulsive behavior that most of us ignore. His goals are fewer and tentatively held. Sometimes his actions are excessive. He is guided by compulsion rather than discipline. He hungers for action and thrives on a situation where the outcome is not known, where he has the freedom to test limits. Of all of the styles the SP works best in crisis situations. He becomes disinterested if there is little variation so may tend to create a crisis to liven things up a bit. He does not wish to save knowledge or accumulate power. He prefers to spend life as freely as possible. Action cannot be saved for tomorrow. Each new day brings need for excitement, adventure, and risk. Resources are to be expended. If you allow your students three tardies per quarter, the SP is apt to use up all three before the third week of the quarter.

The SP is frequently described as exciting, optimistic, cheerful, light-hearted, full of fun. He tends to be charming, witty, and brings an atmosphere of fun charged with adventure and excitement. He is easily bored, must take time out for fun, and enjoys randomness. He can only temporarily be defeated, surviving setbacks well. He acts spontaneously on impulses. He does not have the patience to wait. He has endurance beyond that of others because he is not goal-oriented. Other types are reluctant to exert energy unless there is a reason. The SP does not experience action as duration but simply continues beyond reasonable limits for other types.

One of my own students comes to mind who seemingly is an exact prototype of an SP combination. She ignores classroom rules, is bored very easily, but performs exceedingly well when asked to sing. To relieve some of the symptoms of boredom, I changed her to a more advanced choral ensemble. The pace and performance qualities of that ensemble greatly modified her behavior. In addition, I spent several hours outside of class talking to her only to find out that she was most willing to help with extra things as late into the evening as her parents would allow her to stay. We recently took on the mammoth project of painting our entire choral rehearsal room which had not been painted since 1968. It sounds like a fairly easy task unless you know that everything needed two or three coats of paint. There was a huge balcony that had to be sanded and painted with three coats of paint. Well, our SP prototype, who we will call "Jill," was in the room after school every evening that I would open the room for her to paint. She spent hour after hour working small areas of the room, yet was not anxious to see the room completed. Needless to say, many of my other students and I are very grateful to her for her efforts.

During the time that she was helping with the work on the room, her attitude toward class changed immensely. Once the project was completed she started showing the same attitudes in class that were typical of earlier in the year; however, they are not as often or as pronounced. I continue to search for ways to interest her in the classwork by finding ways to allow her to "perform," such as letting her work one on one with other students who do not have the confidence on their voice part that she does. It helps them to become more secure and at the same time satisfies some of her desire to perform, be noticed, etc.

The SP is often seen as a performer which is a paradox because it takes the discipline of long hours of practice. Once the SP is caught in the hunger action, he will continue long after other types abandon. The impulsive stamina makes virtuosity possible. He seems to be the sole possessor of perfection in action. The NT (intuitive/thinker) seeks perfection but it evades him. The SP is oblivious to the pursuit of perfection. The act in itself realizes perfection. In a sense, the SP does not work, for work implies production, completion, and accomplishment. He is process-oriented. The result is incidental. Work is essentially play. He can sever social ties easily because of his urge to wander. It is not difficult for him to totally abandon everything, yet he is fiercely loyal and willing to share. He usually lives fully in the present and uses whatever resources are available.

One of the most important things to do for an SP student is to vary the class routine as much as possible. The students will not be so aware of an end goal, only that you are working daily on certain activities. Although the students realize that there is an end goal in mind, the SP will not dwell on that fact. At times, you can even do very intense rehearsing on a single piece of music with the SP student because of his ability to stick with something beyond the endurance of most others. He is the type of student that will work very hard on a solo for contest if you do not talk about the deadline of when the solo needs to be prepared or if you do not emphasize the adjudication process. He will improve his own skills tremendously because: one, he can work on something like this for long periods of time; two, he enjoys performing; three, because you have not set his practice schedule other than when he works with you; and four, remember that it is the process which interests him. Often, the time you spend working with this type of student causes him to form a very positive attitude toward you and your classroom.

We will talk a great deal about planning later on. You must plan to include rapid pacing and varied activity in order to appeal to the learning style of the SP. Group activities with the SP as the leader of the group are helpful. Try to include as many different personality temperaments within each group as possible. Make the students aware that you want them to learn to work together and learn to be appreciative of each other's differences.

The **SJ (sensitive/judgmental)** must belong and it must be earned. Dependency is not desired and is not considered legitimate. He feels bound and obligated, not a free spirit like the SP. A strong work ethic is important to him and he is always prepared. He believes in saving for a rainy day. He feels he should earn social hierarchy and has membership hunger, he needs to belong. Tradition becomes more important as he gets older and he has a keen sense for detecting ingratitude. He chooses occupations which involve serving others and belonging to established, recognized institutions.

In any school over half of the teachers pursue the SJ life style. The SJ frowns upon those who stray from the accepted ways. He tends to do the right thing at the right time. His strongest hunger is probably his hunger for belonging. (Kiersey and Bates, 1978)

You can see how the SJ and the SP would have great difficulty in adjusting to a situation where they were forced to work with each other. It is just this kind of discipline that we need to develop within a choral ensemble. We can benefit from the attributes of each, but only when the two different personality types learn to absorb positive elements from each other and learn to tolerate differences. We can begin to develop rapport between the two by having them pair off to do certain classroom exercises, i.e. partners singing scales, one on chromatic, the other on whole-tone. (This was a recommended exercise in the chapter on sight-reading.) Next, we place them in the same group for various cooperative learning activities. An activity we might use in this manner would be to give each group a single line melody that they are to teach to the class without ever demonstrating pitch or rhythm. The group must decide how to present it to the class. This is just one of many ways to vary your method of teaching music literacy skills. We know that one of the best ways to insure our students acquisition of knowledge is to have them teach the material.

The SJ is the type of student that the teacher considers to be the model student. Because of his hunger for belonging, he is compelled to "fit the mold." He feels that breaking the mold will cause his exclusion from the group. His idea is that the main nucleus of the group is formed from those who are willing to do just what the teacher asks most of the time. He does not desire to be singled out as being different. Even if he thinks that his action might please the teacher, although it is a break away from the norm, he often will not take that chance. He is prone to doing things in the usual manner. Teaming him with the SP might encourage him to begin to do some thinking for himself and even allow him to try something of his own creativity that he would not ordinarily try.

Because over half of the teachers in any school do pursue the SJ life style, the SJ student is often considered to be favored by the teachers. Teachers often consider the SJ student to be more cooperative, better disciplined, and maybe even a little brighter than his counterparts. This misconception is derived solely from the appearance of the SJ to always do what the teacher asks rather than the fact that the SJ most likely is of the same personality temperament as the teacher. Instead of looking at other students as a valuable resource in the classroom, we often make the mistake of trying to make all of our students fit one common mold. Many teachers choose teaching as their profession because they are comfortable in that setting where their temperament is much like their peers or colleagues. Our ability to motivate our students is directly proportionate to our ability to make our students feel individually successful. We must learn to tap into their individual personality temperaments in order to help them to become as successful as possible. It requires constant observation, assessment, and planning on our part, not to mention our own self-discipline and patience. This is probably more difficult for the SJ teacher than any of his counterparts since he has been subjected for so long to that style of teaching in many of the classes that he attended as a student.

Let's look at some of the other combinations. Only 12% of the population are **NT's (intuitive/thinking)** Where the SP's and SJ's are constantly surrounded by their own kind, the NT's are not. They seek an entirely different social environment. Power fascinates the NT, power over nature not over people. The NT wants to be able to understand, control, predict, and explain realities. He wants competencies, capabilities, abilities, and skills. He loves acquiring intelligence. He is the most self-critical of all of the styles, causing him to be obsessed with the compulsion to improve. This can also cause him to seem arrogant. He is plagued with self-doubt.

The NT may schedule his play time only to tax himself to improve recreational skills. Often his messages sent to others cannot be comprehended because of the intricacies of ideas discussed. He is seen as unduly demanding because it seems to others that his message is one that dictates they at least attempt to achieve the same level as that which he has self-imposed. It is usually an impossible standard, which causes him to be isolated.

NT's live in their work. Career choices for them are usually in fields such as engineering, architecture, teachers of math and science, and philosophy. They will listen to new ideas and accept them as long as they make sense. They have an inquiring attitude and value things like will, self-control, straight-forwardness in dealing with others. They never are willing to repeat the same error. They can appear to be distant and detached at times.

It must be noted here that one of the prevailing qualities of the NT is his compulsion to improve and the rigidly high standards he sets for himself. Because others around him feel that he expects the same of them, they do not see that he is trying to obtain the same goals for himself. They see him as one who thinks he has already attained such goals and therefore, expects everyone else to follow suit. The outsider feels that the NT's philosophy is one of, "Well, if I can, you should be able too. You just don't want to work as hard as I do, or you just are not as talented as I am." Remember, this is the way the outsider sees the NT, not the way the NT sees himself. The more frustrated the NT becomes with trying to accomplish something, the more arrogant he will seem. His self-doubt leads him into comments like, "Really, it was good? Are you sure? Well, what could I have done better?"

His classmates see this as a way of getting attention. They are not convinced for one moment that the NT senses any degree of failure. The NT will often seem as if he is constantly searching for compliments, when in fact, he is trying to reassure his own self-doubting.

This makes it very difficulty for the NT to be accepted by his peers. Even when he does do something well, his peers are not going to concede that he has, causing more self-doubt. The NT adolescent, like any other adolescent wants desperately to be accepted by his peers. The adolescent age is where peer pressure becomes evident and the desire to fit -in becomes stronger. Decisions made at that age about who the person wants to be, often determine the road that the young person takes. He chooses his friends and their influence guides him for many years to come.

We as teachers also mistake the NT's self-doubt as arrogance. If we can learn to separate self-doubt from arrogance, we can better serve our students. The only way we can determine which is blossoming in an individual student is to get to know him by making an effort to observe him in class more closely. Place him with students where he feels the most comfortable. Perhaps he won't feel that he has to qualify every move to them as often. When he does work on a project, ask him how much time he spent on it, what does he feel he did well on the project. If he had more time to work on the project, what would he try to change? These are all clues as to how much self-doubt he is exhibiting.

The fact that he establishes such high standards for himself can make him an asset to the rest of the group. You can take advantage of this by having him help another student, one on one. Begin by having him explain something to a student who was absent and missed the information. This reaffirms that there is no reason for him to have self-doubt if you entrust another student to him. By having sectional rehearsals in a choral rehearsal, the other students can see and hear for themselves that he does know the part and he is an asset to their section. He almost always is strong because he sets such rigid standards for himself. You can get a positive attitude from the section he is in by complimenting them on the improvement that they made during the sectional rehearsal. They will know where their strength came from and will look at the NT a little differently. They will also get to know him a little better and begin to realize that he is not as arrogant as they once had thought.

Another type that has its own properties is the **NF (intuitive/feeling)**. The goal of the NF cannot be seen as anything other than extraordinary. Consequently, no one can understand his aim. The NF searches constantly for self-actualization, his own uniqueness. The endless search for self causes guilt. He desperately needs to have meaning and wants the significance of any relationship to be appreciated. There must be no facade, mask, or pretense. The NF is extremely sensitive to subtleties in gestures and metaphoric behavior not always visible to other types. He is vulnerable to adding dimensions to communications which are not always shared or perceived by others. As long as some response is shown, the NF will devote a great deal of time and energy to a relationship. More than any other type, the NF can speak and write fluently. He has extraordinary capability to appear to his beholder to be whatever the beholder wants to see.

The NF has great difficulty placing limits on the time and energy he devotes to work because he is always striving for perfection. Once the task is completed, it never lives up to the magnificence of it's conception. NF's place unreasonable demands on themselves and others. It seems to make sense that they probably do not realize that they are placing demands on others. They tend to romanticize experiences because they are focused on what might be. They enjoy bringing out possibilities in others rather than principles.

The best way for the teacher to make the NF feel successful is to show appreciation for his efforts. The NF will often see compliments as falsely bestowed because of his search for perfection. He will see the compliment as the teacher's way of appeasing him to relieve his frustration in his pursuit of impossible perfection. It is very important for the teacher to make certain that compliments are earned and not given freely to the NF. Otherwise, the NF will lose confidence in the teacher and not accept compliments or displays of appreciation that the teacher shows. The same is true of his association with his peers. Integrity must always be the foundation of the positive reinforcement.

Because of the NF's sensitivity to gestures and metaphoric behavior, he tends to be musical in a way that many others are not. It is sometimes easier to get the NF to sing expressively than it is other personality types. He responds very well to subtleties in the conducting gestures, imagery, body movement, and is an excellent candidate for eurhythmics. Give him the opportunity in your class to offer suggestions about what imagery he would use to get a certain sound out of a piece of music or a single phrase. He can present many ideas that would never occur to another individual.

We must constantly remember as teachers that we have all of these wonderful resources at our fingertips because our students are so diverse with their learning styles and personality temperaments. These resources are more valuable than any course we could take. We just have to learn how to use them and stop considering those who differ from our own "ways" as being obstacles.

Children and Indications of Personality Temperaments

Let us take a look at how Kiersey describes these same personality temperament combinations in a child. In so doing, we can better understand the implications of how we can mold the classroom environment to make it more compatible. He describes the **SP child** as active, one who enjoys food, and one who gets into messes. He doesn't understand why rooms need to be clean — he considers that a waste of time. Yet, if inclined, he can become involved in something for hours. This child needs movement and excitement, he hungers for contest.

The SP child will be cheerful in the classroom if frequent change is mingled with some excitement says Kiersey. He enjoys activities, *musical performance*, art, and games. This child appears flighty, jumping from one thing to another, basically because he is disinterested in completion. The more game-like the task, the better. He does not wish to prepare for anything. Although this child likes musical performance, think of the problems this poses for the music teacher who is trying to get a group performance ready. This is where a variety of approaches becomes crucial to the teacher. As for the music teacher, it is where gestures can be invaluable. The less talking and the more activity, the better for this type of student, it would seem. You might lose his attention the minute you stop to tell the choir something, but if he has to watch your gestures for clues, he will remain far more attentive.

Kiersey says that as the demand for concentration increases, the SP child becomes restless and begins to disrupt the class or increases his absenteeism. This child is often labeled, "hyperactive." How often do we hear that in today's society? Although there may be some credence to the suggestion that diets and other changes in society contribute to "hyperactivity," it would be interesting to know which child is truly "hyperactive" and which child simply is an SP type. Kiersey feels that exercises demanding quiet and relaxation must be provided for this child.

He suggests that the SP child must be actively involved in the learning situation as he does not learn well passively. I quote directly from Kiersey, *"The one thing an SP finds holding him in school is the opportunity to play a musical instrument."* He makes this statement because this is one activity that involves both audience and action and on this the SP thrives. Remember, most teachers are SP's even though they pursue the SJ life-style.

The **SJ child** is more vulnerable to family instability than other types. He is only comfortable knowing that what is so today will also be tomorrow. His main source of pleasure is approval of adults when he is assigned specific responsibilities. Because he likes routine, he thrives on clerical methods of teaching (workbooks, repetition, drill, question-answer). The SJ child pleases the teacher. The fact that the teacher asks is sufficient reason. As a learner, he responds best by being shown new skills step by step, being asked to demonstrate each new learning in small increments. This child needs constant feedback from adults because he wants to do things right and please the adults. The SJ child pays attention to small detail, and has high standards of achievement. He is focused on responsibility.

Kiersey suggests that the following ingredients are attractive to the corresponding type:

SJ — programmed learning materials
SP — wants action
NF — wants human interaction
NT — prefers less redundancy

The **NT child** will ask a lot of why questions and will quickly lose respect for those who are not logical in reprimands. Physical punishment is deeply violating to him because dignity is important. He is devastated by ridicule and sarcasm concerning his ability. He is already very self-doubting and needs abundant success for reassurance. He may seem precocious intellectually, but socially slow. NT's usually do not do well in school. Many of them tend to be high achievers but self-doubt gets in the way. A logical presentation of learning materials is apt to appeal to them as well as lectures.

The NT likes directions only once. He is impatient with repetition. The SJ enjoys detailed directions and doesn't mind repetition. The SP doesn't pay much attention to directions, clear or not. The NF erases distinctions in directions and needs both written and oral directions. Independent study works well with the NT.

The **NF child** has a gift for language. He needs and seeks recognition and needs reassurance everyday. Often, an NF child will have an invisible companion because he enjoys his imagination being sparked. He doesn't like competition, so cooperative learning works well. Often hypersensitive, especially INF, he is apt to idolize the teacher. Because he is talented verbally, he usually does well academically. Language is his *forte*, he is good at written and oral communication. He likes to work in small groups. The NF's will conform to the adult expectations if they believe the adults like them. They desperately want to please. They need to be loved. The NF child has difficulty handling anger.

It is very important for the teacher to know this child by name because of his hunger for sense of self and his need for appreciation. The NF child thrives on recognition, personal attention, two-way exchanges, and caring. Personal notes on class work are an excellent motivational tool with this child. Negative reaction can provoke him into rebellion or inaction.

The NF child enjoys interaction, loves group discussions, and is also able to work independently for a time, but needs periodic feedback through dialogue. He learns best through discussion, role-playing, and dramatic plays. Because of his talent in communication skills, his spoken vocabulary is often beyond his ability to put thoughts on paper. If he is allowed to put compositions on audio tape, this is a way to express his richness of creativity.

The **INF (introvert/intuitive/feeling)** is shy (usually no more than one per classroom), hypersensitive to rejection, has a vivid imagination, but may be over-stimulated by violence. He may be subject to nightmares. While so many children love to watch horror films, how do you suppose the INF would react? He prefers cooperation to competition because he identifies so strongly with others. This child prefers subjects that focus on people and learns in face-to-face dialogue. He likes the decision-making of a democratic classroom and enjoys giving pleasure to others. He is very sensitive with his own emotions and towards the emotions of others and consequently, has a built-in drive to better social situations, make them pleasant and nourishing.

The INF children are particularly responsive to teachers who are accepting and nourishing, who verbalize their recognition of feelings, individualize instruction, use lots of small group interaction, who genuinely respond to and accept ideas and opinions of class members, who avoid sarcasm and ridicule as a means of class control. Their empathy toward others will not allow you to use ridicule toward their classmates. Remember, even though INF's comprise only 5% of the population (Bradway, 1964), we draw an unusual amount of them into music classes.

In this chapter I have attempted to summarize the findings of David Kiersey and Marilyn Bates to give the background information necessary for the thoughts behind the rest of this book. This is not intended to be a book on psychology, but some knowledge of the differing learning styles is important if we are to decide on teaching techniques that we want to use. In order to be the best that we can be, it seems only natural that we must learn to teach to the different personality temperaments and not try to mold them into our own way. We can use the resources placed at our fingertips with our varied student population by listening to their suggestions.

The rest of this book will attempt to propose some ways that we can teach to a general population trying to incorporate techniques that will satisfy the different learning styles. I conclude this portion with a quote from the Kiersey and Bates book, <u>Please Understand Me</u>:

"Well, stranger, there isn't any way you can really understand me, but if you stop trying to change me to look like you, you might come to appreciate me. I'll settle for that. How about you?"

I strongly recommend the Kiersey-Bates book to anyone in the teaching profession. I think it can serve as an invaluable tool. They give some interesting statistics about the teaching field. See the chart below.

TEACHING IN STYLE - *Summary*

	Prime Value in Education	% of Teachers / Length of Service	Favored Teaching Areas	Favored Instructional Technique
SPs	Growth of spontaneity and freedom	4% – short stay	arts, crafts, sports, drama, music, recreation	projects, contests, shows, games, demonstrations
SJs	Growth of responsibility and utility	56% – long stay	agriculture, clerical, business, sports, social sciences, political science, homemaking, geography, history	recitation, drill, tests, quizzes, compositions, demonstrations
NTs	Growth of knowledge and skills	8% – medium stay	philosophy, science, communications, mathematics, technology, linguistics	lectures, tests, reports, compositions, projects
NFs	Growth of identity and integrity	32% – long stay	humanities, music, social sciences, foreign languages, theology, theater, speech, political science, homemaking, geography, history	group projects, shows, interaction, games, simulations, discussion

(Kiersey and Bates, p. 166, 1978)

There is a copy of a test in the Kiersey-Bates book that you can take to determine your personality temperament. You can order single copies of the test by sending $.25 a copy to : Prometheus Nemesis Book Company, Post Office Box 2748, Del Mar, C.A., 92014. Ask for, "The Kiersey Temperament Sorter."

We have reprinted that test here with permission from the publisher. You might consider ordering copies from Prometheus Nemesis Book Company to give to your classes so that you have an idea of the balance of personality temperaments within each class. This will give you an idea of your resources and adjustments you might want to make in your teaching style.

Decide on answer a or **b** and put a check mark in the proper column of the answer sheet. Scoring directions are provided on the next page. There are no right or wrong answers since about half the population agrees with either answer you choose.

ANSWER SHEET

Enter a check for each answer in the column for **a** or **b**:

	a	b		a	b		a	b		a	b		a	b		a	b		a	b
1			2			3			4			5			6			7		
8			9			10			11			12			13			14		
15			16			17			18			19			20			21		
22			23			24			25			26			27			28		
29			30			31			32			33			34			35		
36			37			38			39			40			41			42		
43			44			45			46			47			48			49		
50			51			52			53			54			55			56		
57			58			59			60			61			62			63		
64			65			66			67			68			69			70		

1   2   3   4   3   4   5   6   5   6   7   8   7   8

1   2   4   6   8

E   I   **S   N**   **T   F**   **J   P**

Directions for Scoring

1. Add down so that the total number of "a" answers is written in the box at the bottom of each column. Do the same for the "b" answers you have checked. Each of the 14 boxes should have a number in it.

2. Transfer the number in box No. 1 of the answer sheet to box No. 1 below the answer sheet. Do this for box No. 2 as well. Note, however, that you have two numbers for boxes 3 through 8. Bring down the first number for each box beneath the second, as indicated by the arrows. Now add all the pairs of numbers and enter the total in the boxes below the answer sheet, so each box has only one number.

3. Now you have four pairs of numbers. Circle the letter below the larger number of each pair. If the two numbers of any pair are equal, then circle neither, but put a large X below them and circle it.

You have identified your "type." It should be one of the following:

INFP	ISFP	INTP	ISTP
ENFP	ESFP	ENTP	ESTP
INFJ	ISFJ	INTJ	ISTJ
ENFJ	ESFJ	ENTJ	ESTJ

If you have an X in your type, yours is a mixed type. An X can show up in any of the four pairs: E or I, S or N, T or F, and J or P. Hence there are 32 types besides the 16 listed above:

XNTP	EXTP	ENXP	ENTX
XNTJ	EXTJ	INXP	INTX
XNFP	EXFP	ENXJ	ENFX
XNFJ	EXFJ	INXJ	INFX
XSTP	IXTP	ESXP	ESTX
XSTJ	IXTJ	ISXP	ISTX
XSFP	IXFP	ESXJ	ESFX
XSFJ	IXFJ	ISXJ	ISFX

THE KEIRSEY TEMPERAMENT SORTER

1. **At a party do you**
    a. interact with many, including strangers
    b. interact with a few, known to you

2. **Are you more**
    a. realistic than speculative   b. speculative than realistic

3. **Is it worse to**
    a. have your "head in the clouds"   b. be "in a rut"

4. **Are you more impressed by**
    a. principles   b. emotions

5. **Are you more drawn toward the**
    a. convincing   b. touching

6. **Do you prefer to work**
    a. to deadlines   b. just "whenever"

7. **Do you tend to choose**
    a. rather carefully   b. somewhat impulsively

8. **At parties do you**
    a. stay late, with increasing energy
    b. leave early, with decreased energy

9. **Are you more attracted to**
    a. sensible people   b. imaginative people

10. **Are you more interested in**
    a. what is actual   b. what is possible

11. **In judging others are you more swayed by**
    a. laws than circumstances   b. circumstances than laws

12. **In approaching others is your inclination to be somewhat**
    a. objective   b. personal

13. **Are you more**
    a. punctual   b. leisurely

14. **Does it bother you more having things**
    a. incomplete   b. completed

15. **In your social groups do you**
    a. keep abreast of other's happenings
    b. get behind on the news

16. **In doing ordinary things are you more likely to**
    a. do it the usual way   b. do it your own way

17. **Writers should**
    a. "say what they mean and mean what they say"
    b. express things more by use of analogy

18. **Which appeals to you more**
    a. consistency of thought
    b. harmonious human relationships

19. **Are you more comfortable in making**
    a. logical judgments   b. value judgments

20. **Do you want things**
    a. settled and decided   b. unsettled and undecided

21. **Would you say you are more**
    a. serious and determined   b. easy-going

22. **In phoning do you**
    a. rarely question that it will all be said
    b. rehearse what you'll say

23. **Facts**
    a. "speak for themselves"   b. illustrate principles

24. **Are visionaries**
    a. somewhat annoying   b. rather fascinating

25. **Are you more often**
    a. a cool-headed person   b. a warm-hearted person

26. **Is it worse to be**
    a. unjust   b. merciless

27. **Should one usually let events occur**
    a. by careful selection and choice   b. randomly and by chance

28. **Do you feel better about**
    a. having purchased   b. having the option to buy

29. **In company do you**
    a. initiate conversation   b. wait to be approached

30. **Common sense is**
    a. rarely questionable   b. frequently questionable

31. **Children often do not**
    a. make themselves useful enough b. exercise their fantasy enough

32. **In making decisions do you feel more comfortable with**
    a. standards   b. feelings

33. **Are you more**
    a. firm than gentle   b. gentle than firm

34. Which is more admirable:
   a. the ability to organize and be methodical
   b. the ability to adapt and make do

35. Do you put more value on the
   a. definite   b. open-ended

36. Does new and non-routine interaction with others
   a. stimulate and energize you   b. tax your reserves

37. Are you more frequently
   a. a practical sort of person   b. a fanciful sort of person

38. Are you more likely to
   a. see how others are useful   b. see how others see

39. Which is more satisfying:
   a. to discuss an issue thoroughly
   b. to arrive at agreement on an issue

40. Which rules you more:
   a. your head   b. your heart

41. Are you more comfortable with work that is
   a. contracted   b. done on a casual basis

42. Do you tend to look for
   a. the orderly   b. whatever turns up

43. Do you prefer
   a. many friends with brief contact
   b. a few friends with more lengthy contact

44. Do you go more by
   a. facts   b. principles

45. Are you more interested in
   a. production and distribution   b. design and research

46. Which is more of a compliment:
   a. There is a very logical person.
   b. There is a very sentimental person.

47. Do you value in yourself more that you are
   a. unwavering   b. devoted

48. Do you more often prefer the
   a. final and unalterable statement
   b. tentative and preliminary statement

49. Are you more comfortable
   a. after a decision   b. before a decision

50. **Do you**
    a. speak easily and at length with strangers
    b. find little to say to strangers

51. **Are you more likely to trust your**
    a. experience   b. hunch

52. **Do you feel**
    a. more practical than ingenious   b. more ingenious than practical

53. **Which person is more to be complimented: one of**
    a. clear reason   b. strong feeling

54. **Are you inclined more to be**
    a. fair-minded   b. sympathetic

55. **Is it preferable mostly to**
    a. make sure things are arranged   b. just let things happen

56. **In relationships should most things be**
    a. renegotiable   b. random and circumstantial

57. **When the phone rings do you**
    a. hasten to get to it first   b. hope someone else will answer

58. **Do you prize more in yourself**
    a. a strong sense of reality   b. a vivid imagination

59. **Are you drawn more to**
    a. fundamentals   b. overtones

60. **Which seems the greater error:**
    a. to be too passionate   b. to be too objective

61. **Do you see yourself as basically**
    a. hard-headed   b. soft-hearted

62. **Which situation appeals to you more:**
    a. the structured and scheduled
    b. the unstructured and unscheduled

63. **Are you a person that is more**
    a. routinized than whimsical   b. whimsical than routinized

64. **Are you more inclined to be**
    a. easy to approach   b. somewhat reserved

65. **In writings do you prefer**
    a. the more literal   b. the more figurative

66. **Is it harder for you to**
    a. identify with others   b. utilize others

67. Which do you wish more for yourself:
    a. clarity of reason   b. strength of compassion

68. Which is the greater fault:
    a. being indiscriminate   b. being critical

69. Do you prefer the
    a. planned event   b. unplanned event

70.   Do you tend to be more
    a. deliberate than spontaneous   b. spontaneous than deliberate

CHAPTER 3

"Simplifying Concepts
For Expressive Singing"

One of the most difficult tasks we have as choral directors is to teach our students to sing expressively. Whether we communicate with the conducting gesture, demonstrate with our own voice or another instrument, or articulate what we want, the student must understand what we are communicating. If we teach them to depend solely on us for that communication, we have not taught them to think for themselves. We need to also give them an understanding of basic concepts so that they can become intelligent musicians in their own right.

Often because of rigorous performance obligations, we tend to spoon-feed our singers just for the sake of getting ready on time. We are placing ourselves in a "Catch 22" because if we do not take time to educate, we will always have the pressure of time breathing down our neck. If our students have a good foundation from which to make their own musical assessments, our conducting gestures are far more effective, we have to articulate less, and we no longer have the need for constant demonstration. After all, our job is to **educate** and teach our students in a manner that they can make their own musical decisions. It would be a crime to make them dependent on us for those decisions. As was previously stated, *The best favor we can do for our students is to teach them in a manner that allows them to have no need for us.*

Musical expression is probably the one area that we teach our students to be most dependent on us for decisions, perhaps because it is so intangible. The fact that musical expression is not like mathematics makes it difficult to address. Often, there is no right or wrong way, even though performance practices dictate some perameters. Some scores have editorial markings such as tempo, dynamics, *crescendo*, *decrescendo*, etc., but the final decisions are left up to the conductor and/or the performer.

We can teach our singers about musical expression with a few simple concepts by dividing expression into three areas: dynamics, diction, and articulation. We are assuming that vocal production is studied daily so that it is possible for the singer to execute phrases musically once they understand these three concepts of musical expression. It is impossible for a singer to be very expressive if he has poor vocal production. Exercises must be done daily to ensure good vocal health.

Let's explore some ways to narrow down our concepts about good musical expression. In the process, we will try to see how the teaching techniques might be appropriate for the different learning styles. The fewer "rules" we have, the simpler the concept is, the more opportunity we have to exercise that concept or rule in different ways; hence, the more learning styles we can address.

Dynamics

Although most of our students understand what the dynamic markings are telling them to do, they often do not know how to implement what is indicated. In a *forte* section, they will often oversing causing a strident, out-of-tune sound. Likewise, in a *pianissimo* section, they lose the intensity of tone causing airy tone and flatting.

For any given setting, the students must know their vocal limitations. They should sing *forte* only up to what their individual instrument allows without force and stridency. They need to be taught how to sing softly with intensity. Begin by establishing limitations for a given situation, i.e. the rehearsal room, the concert hall, etc.

Instruct the students to sing a normal, healthy, comfortable, energized sound on <u>nah</u>. This will be established as a mezzo *forte* (*mf*) As they sing, write *mf* on the board. Remember, many students are visual learners. Next, tell the students to sing *mf* again, making certain they remember where that sound is in their voice and how it feels; then, ask them to sing one degree louder as you write *f* on the board. Follow the same routine, always going back to the *mf* sound first, increase to *f* and *ff* as you write the *ff*. Ask for increased energy and excitement, rather than increased volume. Asking for more volume often creates stridency of tone, whereas, asking for more energy does not. Remember that we also have students who learn very well with imagery (the intuitives). Using body movement in the classroom will develop coordination and confidence in every student, but it is especially valuable for the intuitive learner. As the students *crescendo* one degree at a time, have them pretend that they are holding books out from their body, waist-high. Insist that they actually "feel" the weight of the books. As they add one degree of volume dynamically, they also add another book or two. Held in this particular position, the "weight" of the books causes the singer to use lower abdomenal muscles in the breathing process. The "sensible" will simply calculate the different degrees of volume that the dynamics indicate. (See Picture 3-1)

Picture 3-1

It is important to feel the proper positioning (first girl) in order to succeed.

Now take the same approach with the exercise to establish the softer sounds. Begin with *mf* again to have a point of reference. The point of reference is the most critical part of setting dynamics. Follow as you did for the forte sounds with *mp*, *p*, and *pp*. The singers now know the "comfort zones" for that particular performance or rehearsal setting. Another exercise my students and I have found successful as we work for a beautiful, intense *pianissimo* sound is to have the singers on an *oo* vowel, and as they sing softer *add more books* to what they are lifting, rather than taking books off of the stack. (Use same imagery as for the *forte* exercise.) The most common mistake the singer makes is to swallow a soft sound. Once again, imagery plays a part. The singer thinks that to keep something soft, he must keep it to himself, so just like the timid introvert, he mumbles and keeps the sound inside the mouth. This is where most of the intensity is lost. The sound must be pulled out of the mouth. Four exercises have been successful for this author.

1.   Hold a paper cup up as you prepare to conduct your choir. Tell them the cup has magic properties and if they will allow you to pull the sound out of their mouth toward the center of the cup, it will be able to work its magic. (See Picture 3-2)

Picture 3-2

Singers "allow" the conductor to pull the sound from them to the center of the cup.

What happens in this exercise is that the visual imagery forces them to place the sound forward in the mouth and the cup causes them to focus on a specific point. That focus also aids in pulling the sound forward.   You can then incorporate the same sort of imagery into conducting gestures. Conductors often ask for a decrease in dynamics by pressing toward the floor with their palms. They may even assume a stooped position to insist on less and less volume. If the gesture is seen as something similar to "pulling the sound out of the mouth" like the exercise above, the sound will be more intense. Try placing your left hand in a stationery position directly in front of you and pulling your right hand slowly back toward you as if you literally are pulling something out of the singers mouth. (See the supplemental video tape for demonstration of this and other techniques.)

2.   As you "pull the sound out of the singers mouth" tell them to let it gradually "soak" into the wall behind you.

You continue with the same conducting gesture discussed in number one, only turn toward the wall behind you and pretend that you are allowing the sound to "soak into the wall" by actually touching the wall.

3. Conduct a *forte* sound on a particular phrase and ask your singers to sing *forte*. Next, tell your singers you are still going to conduct *forte* but you want them to sing *pianissimo*. Finally, conduct *pianissimo* and see if they can execute a phrase with intensity.

4. Have the singers form as large a circle as they can by interlocking their hands in front of them; then, have them sing into that circle and put as much energy into the immediate circle as is possible for each individual. (See Picture 3-3)

Picture 3-3

Greet the musical phrase outwardly. Do not keep it to yourself.

Singers can only fill up so much space. Of course, projection helps. If you tell the young singer to fill up the auditorium with sound, you are probably going to get mostly air and forced sound. By having the singers try to place as much energy as possible into the circle they have formed with their hands, they get much more intensity because they are listening more for the correct sound (vocal production) and they are not forcing. To them, it is possible to fill that amount of space with good, energetic sound, so they concentrate on the task and have more success.

Use the canon "Himmel und Erbe" (page 30) and begin the 1st phrase *mf*, 2nd phrase *f*; etc. to establish dynamic levels. Follow this with using other phrases of the canon to decrease dynamic levels. The most important thing is to establish where the mf level should be in order to make all other dynamic levels work successfully.

Singers cannot produce what they have not heard or experienced. In order to hear what a good *crescendo* or *decrescendo* should sound like, the director needs to let the choir experience that sound. Since young singers do not immediately have the vocal production to produce a good *crescendo* or *decrescendo*, we must find other ways to show them what we are aiming for.

Let's assume that we are using a piece that has an "MGM" ending with grandiose *allargando*, *forte*, and a *crescendo* that goes forever. The young singer is unable to pace and use his voice in a situation of this sort without putting undo stress on the vocal cords. He sees the markings in the score, we get excited conducting, and the singer gives everything possible to *crescendo* without letting up or taking a breath for the entire four measures of tied whole-notes that end with a *fermata*! One way to approach this problem is to have the choir number off in "fours" in each section. Tell the "ones" to *crescendo* only for the duration of the first whole-note and hold at that dynamic level, getting a breath wherever needed. The "twos" do not begin to *crescendo* until the second whole-note and continue only during the duration of it, the "threes" on the third whole-note and the "fours" on the final whole-note. On the *fermata* the conductor can then indicate the final *crescendo* for all four numbers so that the one last big increase in dynamics is heard right up to the final cut-off.

A variation of this might be called for if you wanted to hear certain chord colors. You might want the basses to *crescendo* on the first note (the more lows we hear in a choral sound, the better the opportunity for over-tones), the altos on the second, tenors on the third, and sopranos on the fourth. In order to help breath-management, you can use numbers in the same manner by having the students write in their score what number breathes at which place in the text. Sometimes staggered breathing does not solve the problem of long phrases when the number method does.

We can use the same principle for *decrescendos* or *pianissimo* passages. With the inexperienced singer it sometimes helps to have singers drop out at certain points until the ensemble understands what type of sound you are trying to achieve. Follow the same procedure as for the *crescendo* by having the "ones" *diminuendo* until the end of the first whole-note, hold their mouth in a position that looks as if they are still singing, but stop making sound by the time they reach the second whole-note. Follow suit for the other numbers. This will illicit a beautiful effect and the audience does not realize how it is achieved if the students act like they are singing all the way to the final cut-off. A variation of this technique would be to have the singers perform in quartets rather than in sections. As was previously discussed, arrange the choir so that the best blending voices are placed in the center. In order to give the effect of a beautifully controlled de*crescendo*, start by conducting with palms up, hands apart as if you are trying to include the entire choir (one hand toward each end of the risers), slowly move hands to the center as if you are pulling the sound to the middle of the choir while it is gradually getting softer. As your hands pass each group of singers on the risers, they pretend to sing but stop making sound immediately after your hands pass them. As you pull to the middle of the choir, that core keeps singing and you finish the *diminuendo* by "pulling the sound from their mouth" as was discussed earlier. (Suggestion number 2, page 52)

Sometimes, to get a singer to focus the tone so that *pianissimo* sections have more intensity, the same principle can be applied as was suggested with the paper cup. Either draw a small flower on the board or put a picture of one where it is visible to the entire choir and ask the choir to sing with enough energy to make the flower blossom fully, but softly enough that it will not disturb or bruise the petals. To the "thinking" personality temperament, this will seem absurd! The "intuitive" personality temperament will really get into an exercise like this. The "sensibles" will latch onto the number system explained above, very readily. ***Remember, we are constantly searching for ways to attract both types of learning styles.*** It is great fun to see how the students react differently to the diversity of these exercises. Making those of one learning style experiment with something that is so opposing to their natural "comfort zones" is good discipline. Each eventually learns to appreciate the capabilities of the other and gains new levels of understanding. It is much more difficult for the "sensible" to adjust to some of these exercises than it is the "intuitive," but they usually enjoy watching each other and can't help but to become involved when their peers seem to latch onto something that is so foreign to them.

Many of these techniques are not to be confined to the specific examples given but can be used in many different ways. For instance, singing into the paper cup or singing to the flower can also be used to get a particular vowel shaped and focused. Vowel placement is often hampered with the soft palate being dropped. A bit of imagery we can use to help that problem is to ask the singer to pretend to sip a soda through a straw. First, sip the soda as if he is extremely thirsty and only gets to

Picture 3-4

Notice how each mouth position is exaggerated with use of elastic. The singer on the left is pulling down too much causing chest tone placement. The singer in the middle is using horizontal placement. The singer on the right is pulling upward from the waist—acheiving desired vertical placement by the vowel.

have as much soda as he can accumulate from one sip. Pay attention to what kind of feeling there is in the back of the throat. Next, sip through the straw as if trying to get a very thick chocolate milk-shake through it only to have the straw collapse. Feel the difference of what occurs in the back of the throat. With the soda, the soft palate "lifts." The milk-shake causes it to "pull down." Many young singers collapse the soft-palate in an effort to reach high tones. They squeeze it as if it were the opening to a balloon. So often, we just say, "open the throat." That attention to the throat causes the singer to tighten by trying to manipulate the musculature surrounding the throat. Sometimes, the more we draw attention to the problem area, the larger the problem becomes because of tension. If we find other ways to approach the problem without drawing attention directly to the problem area, we may be more successful. For this reason, the exercise of simply "sipping through a straw" may be more effective with lifting the soft palate than talking about an open throat. For the sensibles, we simply explain that as we pretend to be sipping, the soft palate lifts as it should when we sing. That is enough to suffice for them but not for everyone. (See picture 3-4)

Another example of drawing attention to the problem is trying to get the singer to open the mouth more. We say things like, "drop the jaw, open your mouth, sing with three fingers in your mouth, etc." In most of these instances, it will be overdone, causing tension. Particularly, if we say, "drop the jaw." To the young singer this means *push* the jaw down. Anytime there is a push-down motion, the soft-palate is pulled down in the process. Pushing the jaw down pulls all of the facial muscles down causing tension. The nasal passages should feel as if you just took a big whiff out of an opened jar of mentholated Vicks. That sort of "lifted" feeling should be felt above the jaw rather than everything being drawn downward. The face needs to have animation and expression. The eyes must be used for expression. In order to avoid the tension caused by pushing the jaw down, say, "lift the top, back teeth," instead of "drop the jaw." We also can create an image with our own facial expression as conductors. If you have ever watched Helmuth Rilling conduct, his facial expressions are wonderful! He is also an extraordinary mime.

The "inside smile" that Ms. Henderson describes in her book "How to Train Singers" is another good way to get the desired results. She explains it as the smile that you are trying not to let anyone see, the hidden smile on the inside and not the outside of the mouth. This provides the adequate space on the inside of the mouth for resonance of correct vocal production. There are many ways to approach the everyday problems that all of us experience. If you have some absolute jewels, make sure you share them with someone. We all are searching for new ideas all the time. (See pictures 3-5 and 3-6)

Picture 3-5

Biting an apple, sniffing mentholatum help achieve animated facial space without tension.

Picture 3-6

For correct vowel formation, the apple must be approached with the upper rather than lower teeth.

Another vocal exercise that I use to show the singer's that they are in control of their soft palate is as follows: sing *kuh - ng - uh* on a single pitch. The *kuh* sound provides a reflex action that lifts the soft palate high. The *ng* sound allows it to drop, the *uh* then lifts it again, showing the singer he is in control. He also begins to understand the difference in the feeling of a dropped versus a lifted soft palate. We often have to show a singer how something feels when it is wrong in order to know how it feels when it is correct. See **Example 10**.

Example 10

Kuh - ng - uh

Another exercise I recommend for both breath control and dynamic control: sing a single pitch on a neutral vowel for sixteen counts. Begin *pianissimo* and gradually *crescendo* for the first eight counts and *decrescendo* for the next eight counts. Increase the exercise in increments of two up to thirty-two counts. If you want to add a good ear-training challenge to this exercise, crescendo for the first eight as you gradually raise the pitch one-half step during the course of the eight counts. Next, do the exercise by beginning *forte* instead of *pianissimo*. This is important because many singers automatically sharp as they <u>increase</u> the dynamic level. This will help break that habit. Do the same exercise moving the pitch down one-half step. You can also add body movement as we did on the chromatic scale. (Palms down, place one hand on top of the other, gradually raise the elbow of the arm that has the hand on top while you lower the pitch one-half step) This is a reminder of good breath support as was explained in the section on sight-reading. It also is a visual way to remind the singer not to make the distance too wide. (See Picture 3-7)

Picture 3-7

Begin with hand rested as shown by the young man, then lift the elbow as shown by the young woman.

Vocal technique must coexist with all other techniques used for expressive singing. You cannot teach a young singer how to use dynamics with finesse until he has mastered the vocal technique required for that kind of control. Any facet of expressive singing demands certain degrees of vocal technique. Because vocal technique and degrees of expression are synonymous, they must be taught simultaneously. For this reason, it is important not to tell a student to simply sing *forte*, but explain how to sing *forte* with correct vocal production. Since he is not going to learn correct breathing or vowel placement in one easy lesson, we find ways to accomplish certain sounds without sacrificing or damaging the youthful instrument. We allow them to mature into an expressive sound by showing them what we eventually want something to sound like, but without asking them to produce something for which their voice is not ready. This is why we use "gimmicks" if you choose to call them that, to get *fortes* and *pianissimos* to sound a certain way. The most important job we have is to keep our singers voices healthy and that means we show them how to take care of their instrument. They can't go out and buy a new one if they wear theirs out!
(See Picture 3-8)

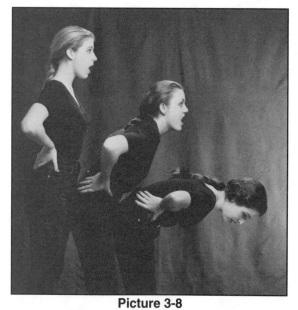

Picture 3-8

Begin inhalation in the lowest position with hands on lower back. Keep inhaling as you move to the tallest position

Summary

Remember, our beginning objective was to narrow down our concepts. To make the concept of dynamics as simple as possible, remind your students of the initial exercise where you established *mf* and then *crescendoed* and *decrescendoed* one degree at a time. We began with an *mf* because it is a comfortable, energetic sound. We then relate all other dynamics to this *mf*, each student finding their individual limitations of *forte* and *pianissimo*. Of course, we remind them of the indications of the dynamic markings in the musical score and insist that they respond without being told. Finally, always make them aware of doing only what their personal good vocal health will allow them to do, regardless of what the conductor asks of them.

Diction

Once again, we need very few "rules" in order to develop techniques that promote good diction. By insisting that the singers follow these "rules" in every piece of music, they soon get into good habits and save the teacher time by not having to go over every word in each phrase. Simplicity is the key to presenting material that we want the students to remember and apply to the musical score.

We will begin by attacking the most common errors made by the young singer. It is understood that vibrant, resonant tones cannot be produced without good breath energy, so we will assume that exercises are being conducted in each rehearsal to develop those habits. Here we will discuss the ways that good diction can enhance rich tone production and add energy to the musical line.

1. **All syllables of the text must be held for the rhythmic duration indicated, on a pure vowel sound.**

The most common error made and perhaps the hardest one to correct with any inexperienced singer, is closing to the consonant of any given syllable or word too soon. Holding out the vowel sound causes the singer to produce much more sound and there is the danger of being heard over other singers if they all choose to close to the consonant more quickly. Most inexperienced singers are very fearful of their voice being heard above those of other singers. There is safety in being the first to close the vowel sound by going to the consonant. Of course, going to the consonant early means that the notes are not held out for their full value. It also means that the singer does not have to keep the breath energy flowing as long. All young singers feel safety in numbers and would die rather than be the sole person to be heard.

That is one of the reasons this is such a common error and therefore a concept that must be taught. No singer is naturally going to hold onto a pure vowel sound without being made aware that it is the proper way to produce sound. We do not use normal speech patterns in this manner and any inexperienced singer is going to sing the same way he speaks unless he is trained differently.

There are several exercises we can do to develop good habits of singing on the vowel. A very effective exercise that I use is shown on **Example 11.**

Example 11

Zing-a- mah mah, zing-a-mah mah, zing-a-mah mah,zing- a-mah mah, zing,zing, zing.

The idea of this exercise is to refrain from going to the *ng* of *zing* for as long as possible. Also the movement from the *ee* vowel in *zing* to the *ah* vowel of *mah* causes the singer to first form a very naturally bright vowel in the mouth, followed by a vowel that is a bit more difficult to keep from swallowing. Many young singers will have a tendency to pull the top lip down over the teeth causing the *ah* vowel to be pulled back into the throat too far. The vowel loses intensity and becomes swallowed. If a young singer can be taught to sing an *ah* vowel with a bright, energetic sound, most other vowels can be related to it. Encourage the singer to lift the top back teeth, let the top lip remain in a natural, relaxed position rather than pulling it down over the top teeth, and keep an "open" face, by feeling a slight lift of the eyebrows. (Too much lift of the brows will cause tension in the face.)

Next the singer should be encouraged to sing the *ee* vowel tall in the mouth like the *ah* rather than pinched and horizontal. Finally, concentrate on the *ng* and make certain that the word *zing* is produced by stretching out the *zee* sound in the word rather than the *ng* sound becoming dominant. Better use of breath energy will be induced by having the singer first practice singing the last three notes of the exercise with pulsated breathing technique. (**Example 11A**)

Example 11A

The second vowel sound of a diphthong should be treated as a consonant. The same delay should occur as it does with initiating the final consonant. For instance, in the word *day*, the *deh* should be held until the release with a breath or movement to the next word. The final *ee* should then be placed on the word. Most of the time, the diphthong must be thought of as a double consonant such as in the word *plate* which would be sung *pleh - eet*.

Another good exercise for developing sustain on the vowel sound is singing entire pieces or phrases on nothing but vowels. Sing "America" with nothing but pure vowel sounds. Most of the words are produced with an *ah* or *ee*. Once this is established and the piece is sung with pure vowels successfully, insert the consonants without disrupting the flow of the vowels.

For our intuitive friends, we can describe this technique with imagery in the following way:

Think of the vowels as being a stream of water pouring out of a faucet. The consonants want to "cut through" the stream of water without interrupting the flow. Pass your hand through the water quickly and precisely. If you let your hand linger too long under the water, the water will splash in your face. We want our musical phrases to be clean and flowing, not "splashed." We want to take all of the "bumps" out of the phrase by executing the phrase with beautiful vowels, only inserting the consonants for clarification of the text and energy within the phrase with ***no interruption of the phrase***. All vowels should be sung "very tall" in the mouth. Often, I will indicate this by drawing an "ah" vowel on the board in these two different manners:

ah ————————— AH

Consonants

With beginning consonants, we want to teach the singer to get through the consonant as quickly as possible and produce the sound of the pitch with the vowel. Let an *l* be a surprise to the mouth instead of allowing the tongue to linger too long at the roof of the mouth. The letter *s* is often difficult to get the precision we want out of an entire choir or ensemble. Whenever possible, if a word ends in *s* do not take a breath before singing the next word of the phrase. This will prevent the choir from sounding like snakes hissing because alleviating the breath will make certain that all singers put the *s* on the end of the word at the exact same time. In order to get the singers to place an *s* on the end of a word with precision, have them practice an exercise like this: sing an *s* for the duration of a whole note, then two half-notes, next four quarter notes, eight eighth-notes, finally an eighth-note followed by an eighth-rest. Say the five measures at a tempo that will make the *s* sound as if it were staccato when you get to the measure of eighth-notes followed by eighth-rests. See Exercise 12.

Example 12

SS,   SS,   SS,   SS, SS, SS, SS,   SS, SS, SS, SS, SS, SS, SS, SS,   SS,   SS,   SS,   SS.

Another exercise is to use the paper cup as we did to get an intense ***pp*** sound (page 51). This time, as you are "pulling" the sound toward the inside of the cup, tell the singers to place the final *s* on the word at the instant that you tap the cup. You must display a preparatory gesture as a prelude to the "tap."

This leads us to our next diction rule. The second rule must also be emphasized and insisted upon with singers. Because we Americans are very lazy with our speech patterns; seldom do we pronounce our consonants cleanly, if we pronounce them at all.

2. Purposely pronounce beginning and final consonants.

This has to be exaggerated with the inexperienced singer because the natural tendency is to "fall into" a word and then leave that same word without paying any attention to the final consonant. No matter what else may be done to get the energy into the music, without the consonants being pronounced very precisely and at the precise time that the musical score indicates, the music will lack some of the vitality and energy that the consonants are so noted for producing. Care must be taken as we work with our students to pronounce the consonants though, not to break rule number one. As we begin to work on consonants, the singer will momentarily go back to habits of closing to the consonant too soon in order to make certain that it is placed on the word or syllable. Part of this problem is caused when the consonants are not short and crisp enough, especially words ending in *s*, *p*, *t*, and *k*.

We have discussed the *s* above, so we will do an exercise this time with the other three letters. Begin by having the singers make the *p* sound by "popping" their lips together. Avoid "pushing" air through the lips so that there is a lingering puff of air sounding as the letter is pronounced. This extra air not only is a waste of breath energy and management, the letter *p* is heard only as a rush of air rather than a letter, especially when you have several singers trying to sing it at the same time. A tremendous amount of energy in the word is lost. Next, "pop" the *t* sound at the roof of the mouth, directly behind the teeth. Again, avoid the rush of air that is often produced with this sound.

Finally, "pop" the *k* sound in the upper part of the throat without excess air. This will train the singer to place final consonants on with exactness. The avoidance of the extra puff of air following the consonant by "imploding" rather than "exploding" will make certain that the final consonant is not only heard, it will be more precise and rhythmically energetic. Although there may be times when we do not want the consonant this short, we are trying to attack the most common problems of the inexperienced singer. Any "rule" that we decree shall be followed may be broken occasionally if it is apropos to the musical score. We are setting down foundations to be adhered to for the majority of the time. For instance, if we were to sing the word, ***"Kyrie,"*** we would not want to "pop" the *k* sound. In that particular instance, we simply would disrupt the flow of the word.

Not only does the above exercise serve to produce cleanly executed consonants, it will enhance singing *pianissimo* by adding energy. Have the choir speak, "Peter Piper picked a peck of pickled peppers." You will hear a great deal of air at the beginning of each word. Try again and insist that all of the beginning consonants are "popped" in the mouth instead of forced out of the mouth with air. Once the consonants become clean, say the phrase a few more times striving for the softest distinguishable sound. Let your singers know that singing *pianissimo* with **intensity** is dependent not only on dynamics, but also on diction. If your students do not understand the word intensity, have them pair off in "twos" to do this quick exercise: first, have one singer place his hand under the hand of the other singer, palms up. Next, have the singer with the bottom hand push the hand of the other singer upward with no resistance from him. Then, have the singer with the top hand, turn palm down and push down as the other singer tries to push his hand upward. This resistance by the upper hand is an excellent example of **intensity**. Again, we are allowing for those who remember things in a different way from some of their peers. We must provide visuals for those who need them.

Now that we have talked so long about consonants, let's talk about the words that begin with vowels. Our third diction rule will read as follows.

3. Every word must have its own, clean beginning.

This applies mainly to those words beginning with vowel sounds. However, the singer sometimes will even elide words that begin with consonants. For instance, the phrase, "the child is not" will sound like "the child is snot" if there is no conscious awareness of preventing the elision of the *s* into the beginning of *not*. Most of the time, we need only to pay special attention to the words that begin with vowels. It is almost certain that the singer will elide the final consonant of a word that precedes one beginning with a vowel into the beginning of that word. Think about common errors like "round John virgin." It is much easier to elide a final consonant into the next word to maintain a *legato* sound than it is to develop good enough vocal technique to make the beginning of each word sound cleanly without disrupting the flow of the line. It must happen so quickly that there is no interruption, very much like what we talked about with the stream of water and our hand cutting through it. In the chapter on articulation we will see how the "Rules of Articulation" work hand-in-hand with the "Rules of Diction" to make this possible.

Our next rule of diction has to do with how we perform double consonants contained in a word.

4. If a word contains a double consonant within it, sing only the second one and omit the first. (This does not apply to languages that require both consonants to be sounded, such as Italian.)

A good example of this would be the word, "alleluia." The first syllable is often closed to the *l* too soon causing it to sound like a man's proper name. If we simply have the singer mark through the first *l* indicating its omission, we will get the *ah* that we anticipated. This is one word that is the same in almost every language. If we take the Latin form of it, we know that the second syllable would not have the diphthong present in a long a sound. We would say it as if it were the word *lay* but without moving to the diphthong *ee* sound. Another Latin phrase that often uses a word that produces a very nasal sound is, "et in terra pax." The word *terra* becomes nasal when the first syllable is spoken or sung with too much *r* sound. This problem also is eliminated by simply omitting the first *r* and pronouncing only the one on the second syllable of the word.

This leads us to our fifth rule of diction.

5. Move all r's over to the beginning of the next word or the next syllable of a word.

This does not mean that we break our rule of elision which we have previously discussed. It simply means that we only put a hint of *r* on a word rather than dwelling on it. Let's go back to the canon that was shown on page 30. ("Himmel und Erde") If we use the English text, look at the word "perish." Sing the word as it is divided syllabically — *per-ish*. Now use our fifth diction rule and sing the word with the *r* moved over to the next syllable — *pe-rish*. Listen to how much better the vowel placement is and how much more sophisticated the language sounds.

Some people say that if you tell the students to simply omit the r at the end of a word, enough of them will forget that it will be just about right. I personally have some reservations about this approach. For one thing, that is giving our students license to "forget" or "ignore" what we tell them to do. Secondly, getting them in the habit of leaving consonants off of a word does nothing to help us reinforce what we said in rule #2 where we asked our students to become very conscious of purposely putting beginning and final consonants on the words. Of course, in the end, when we have the pressure of performances, we all will do whatever is necessary to get the intended affect of the text or to make the text understood. Personally, I feel that I have the responsibility of trying the approach first of how much *r* and when should it be placed in the text.

Let's briefly summarize the five rules of diction and show how we could then examine possible ways to mark our score as reminders to our students as they develop good diction habits.

Rules Of Diction

1. **All syllables of the text must be held for the rhythmic duration indicated, on a pure vowel sound.**

2. **Purposely pronounce beginning and final consonants.**

3. **Every word must have its own clean beginning. (Do not elide one word into the next.)**

4. **If a word has a double consonant within it, sing only the second one and omit the first. (This does not apply to languages that require both to be sounded, such as Italian.)**

5. **Move all r's over to the beginning of the next word or the next syllable of a word.**

Below are shown some of the ways the text to a musical score can be marked by the singer until the diction rules have become habit. On rule number one, if the singer comes across a word where the tendency to close the vowel too soon exists (such as one ending in *ng, n,* or *m*), two things can be marked. First of all, simply write the vowel sound under the word. Next, mark the interfering consonant in the following manner to serve as a reminder to hold it off longer before closing to its sound (sing = sing). Rule number two can be indicated by simply underlining or circling the consonants. To become more exact, the singer must also be taught that final consonants occurring where a breath is to be taken or on a rest, are placed right on the breath or rest when the conductor's gesture so indicates. Those places where it may not be easy or even feasible for the conductor to indicate the breath each time (such as for each voice part in polyphony or when the breath occurs on the off-beat) it will help to have the singer mark the score indicating exactly where the consonant should be placed. We need to *make our students responsible singers*. Most of the time the singer should be solely responsible for remembering to do something without the aid of a reminder from the conductor. If we do not insist that our singers become responsible in this manner, they will not. They will remain dependent on us as long as we allow it. See the following excerpt from Bach's *Cantata 142.*

It would be very easy and convenient to simply place the *d* of *God* right on the third beat where the quarter rest occurs, but try something before making that decision. Try putting that *d* on the and of two instead of on three. This does two things:

1. The singers diction is cleaner because the *d* is shortened to fit into the second half of a beat rather than using a whole count.

2. The consonant causes the finality of the phrase to have more energy because of its pointedness and the fact that it falls on an off-beat. People like the energy in jazz because of its strong attachment to off-beat accents.

For rule number three, we simply remind ourselves not to elide one word into the next by placing a slash mark between the two, i.e. dream/a dream. In order to adhere to rule number four, we simply mark through the first letter of the double consonant leaving only the second visible, i. e. al- le - lu - ia. We remind ourselves to move the *r* over as we did with moving over final consonants that might cause premature closure: (man - ge r).

Articulation

This is the area of expressive singing that seems to be the most difficult for the young singer to grasp. Well-articulated phrases have more influence on the overall expressiveness of the musical score than any other factor. Again, it goes without saying that this aspect of developing musical qualities is co-dependent on good vocal technique. However, developing a good sense of phrasing will increase the expressive qualities of any singer more than any other single ingredient and at the same time enhance whatever vocal technique the singer has acquired. Good vocal technique is automatically developed as the singer learns to execute tasteful phrasing.

Let's define what we mean by the term, "articulation." The word includes everything that has to do with the manner in which a phrase is executed. It is the kind of attack that is used for each note and how each note relates to the other notes and rests in the phrase. It is the manner in which each phrase is prepared and connected to phrases which precede and follow it. Every single note will be taken into consideration as we decide how to best form note groupings to enhance the shape of the phrase. Phrases must have points of renewal within themselves to keep them from becoming stagnant and to allow forward motion to the next phrase.

Without an understanding of good phrase articulation, emotion in the music cannot be brought out to the point that the listener and performer experience the kind of excitement that is possible. Since some of the qualities of good musical expression seem so intangible, our students become far more dependent on us for direction. Many times we say things like, "Sing that phrase more musically." Maybe some of our students have the innate ability to comply, most do not. We then become dependent on a few of our students to demonstrate to the rest or we demonstrate with our own voices. Both of these approaches may serve us well much of the time, but what kind of musical intellect are we developing in our students if we do not give them some concrete concepts from which to make their assessments?

The "intuitive" student may well be able to respond to the statement, "Sing more musically," or even be able to learn by listening to other students. It may not be so easy for the "sensible" student who needs something more concrete. It is just not enough to tell our students to "sing musically." We must be able to explain, demonstrate, and instill some concepts which will aid them in making future musical decisions about phrasing.

We will begin by coming up with a set of rules for articulation that are suitable for any style of music, then we will decide how strongly and when we should implement each rule or concept. This will vary to some degree depending on the style of the music. Finally, we will see how these rules of articulation and note groupings enhance the properties of good diction. We will see how articulation, dynamics, and diction work as one entity.

At all times we must remember that singing musically is a result of *preparing the phrase*. All singing is a series of preparations. Whether we think in terms of conducting an ensemble or singing with an ensemble, we must always think about preparing the phrase so that each note has its function in developing the musical expression of the score. Each note or rest sets up what is to follow. The music loses its expressive qualities when things happen suddenly, without leading up to or falling away from the shape of the phrase. Most of the time, we do not want a sudden *forte* or *pianissimo*. We must set it up by gradually letting each note lead us there. Within the phrase, there needs to be constant tension and release. If we have constant tension or constant relaxation, the music becomes stagnant. Its like anything else in life. We become bored with something always being the same. The music loses its forward motion when we do not reach and pull, relax, then reach and pull again.

In order to avoid mechanically produced phrases where we gradually *crescendo* to the climax of the phrase, and *diminuendo* after the climax, we will set up **Rules of Articulation** which will provide tension and release or relaxation within the phrase. This will energize all movement within the phrase and give forward motion to the music. Phrasing is much more dependent on these renewals than it is the simple *crescendo, decrescendo* process. Without renewing the energy throughout the phrase, we do not feel or hear the climax. We simply hear "measures" of music that at some point become louder, then softer.

The music "stops" every measure because the bar line has become a signal as to where the strong and weak beats always fall. The strong beat of a given time signature has been ingrained in each of us since our first introduction to the world of music. We have practiced emphasizing the strong beats of measures since day one. This habit insures that the music will have a sense of "stopping" at the end of each measure. We must still be aware of the strong beats, but must put more thought into how we will prepare its strength in relation to the rest of the phrase. It simply is a matter of preparing the strong beat with the note that precedes it rather than landing on the strong beat.

The crusis, or downbeat, of a measure is always strong. Think of the crusis as stepping up to a step. The placement of your foot on the step without preparing is impossible. You prepare by first lifting your foot above the step and *then* placing your foot onto the step. You actually relax as you let your foot fall onto the step (See Pictures 3-9 and 3-10). Preparing the crusis is much the same process. You "lift" the note preceding the crusis by putting a little extra energy or weight on it and then "stretch" into the crusis by elongating it slightly to give the sense of it being the strong beat. There is actually more energy placed on the preparation note than on the strong beat.

Picture 3-9

The crusis should have this feeling of landing in place.

Picture 3-10

The crusis often is approached in this harsh manner.

The climax of the phrase is much like the energy used by the pole-vaulter. In order to get the lift necessary to reach proper height for vaulting over the pole, all thought and energy must be placed in the preparation. The height is decided by the energy used in the run preceding the vault and finally, the energy and force with which the pole is placed onto the ground to push upward. We will think of the insertion of the pole into the ground and the push which follows as being the same energy that must be placed on the preparation note or rest. Sometimes, the rest must be the energizing force. The music becomes much more rhythmic because of the energy in that rest. In such a case we might say something like, "Make that the loudest rest that you haven't sung." That tells the singers how much emphasis should be placed on the energy of that rest. In the **Rules of Articulation** that follow, these same ideas will become the general philosophy of establishing the rules and setting forth ideas of note groupings.

First of all, let's set some guidelines and general understandings. We will refer to the energized or preparation notes as being "accented." These are not accents in the true sense. Rather than perform the note with a percussive attack, we will energize with a "lift." The note is simply given more attention by applying a little extra energy and weight. For the thinker we will have to explain by showing that an accent indicates this kind of an attack, whereas, a lift means we put a little *crescendo* on the note once we have initiated sound rather than being so forceful on the attack. We can also indicate where we want those lifts in the score with our conducting gestures. For instance in ¾ time signature, we will indicate the "lift" of count three into count one by "dragging" that third count gesture in a tenuto fashion into count one. (like the gesture used to meld a beat)

Second, it is understood that all notes that are "accented" belong with what follows them and not what is before them. Since we have already talked so much about the last count of a measure preparing the downbeat of the next measure, we will use it as our example. In ¾ time, the third count of the measure would be phrased or grouped with the next measure rather than being grouped with the other two counts of its own measure as the barline indicates. Remember, before music notation was developed into what we consider modern notation, there were no barlines. Think about the two measures of "America" where the text is "Sweet land of liberty." Most singers sing it as follows:

Sweet land of lib - er- ty,

They would automatically accent the "Sweet" and "lib." Put the "accent" or renewal on the word "of," group that word with "liberty" in the next measure, stretching "lib" to show that it is the strong beat of the measure and also the strong syllable of the word. Listen to the difference. The latter way is far more musical. While we are still looking at this part of the score, we want to handle the "b" of "liberty" as we do "r's." (Diction rule #5). Move it over to the next syllable. [li - be(r - ty]

We are going to direct our thoughts now toward the exact **Rules of Articulation** with explanations and examples of each. These "rules" are presented in sequential order according to what this author feels from experience is the best order to follow in introducing them. Some of them produce more instantaneous results than others. *Remember, feelings of success bring about desires for more knowledge.* For this reason, we will use the "rules" first that will bring the most apparent changes in expressiveness.

Rules Of Articulation

1. Never accent the last note of a phrase or the last syllable of a word.

Listen to any young choir sing a piece before the director has discussed shaping with them. The singers will automatically pounce on the last note of a phrase. This is commonly the most unmusical practice singers exhibit. Unless singers are taught to take pressure off of the last note of a phrase, they will almost always land with tension.

Mycoun-try 'tis of thee, sweet land of lib - er- ty, of thee I sing.

It is not as common for a young singer to accent the last syllable of a word as it is a single syllable word, but it does happen on words like, "alleluia," or "liberty," as seen in "America." Look at the "Alleluia" (Bach-Kuhnau) from Bach's **Cantata 142**.

The untrained singer is automatically going to put more weight on the "ia" than any other syllable of the word. It is also the last note of the phrase in this case, but often the word "alleluia" is handled the same way whether or not it is the last note of the phrase. Try re-grouping the notes of the Bach in the following manner:

The strong syllable of the word is "lu." This way, we keep the forward motion throughout the phrase and the text is executed as a single word rather than alle, luia. Remember, we are going to delete the first "l." (Al - le - lu - ia)

2. All phrases begin where the previous one left off.

This second rule of articulation is attacking one of the most common faults of the inexperienced singer. Because he has breath for increased breath energy and management at the beginning of the phrase, he usually will enter at least one dynamic degree louder than he ended with on the previous phrase. This breaks the continuity of moving from one phrase to another and like the barlines, separates the music into phrases now instead of measures. We use notes and rests to prepare the shape of the phrases and we use phrases to prepare the shape of the piece. Each phrase must now prepare the next just as we did with the notes and rests.

First, we must always remember to begin a phrase where the previous one has left off, unless of course the composer has asked for a sudden change.

Next, we must remember to use the last note of a phrase as a set up for the beginning of the next phrase. You may think that this contradicts what we just said in rule one about the last note of a phrase, but it really does not. We are trying to prevent a harsh attack and emphasis on that last note.

Let's look at a few ways a new phrase might begin. First, it will serve as a continuation of the previous phrase and in that case, we simply relax the end of the first phrase, sing gradually softer as we approach the cadence. The next phrase simply begins at the same dynamic level with which we ended the previous phrase. Next, let's say we have a phrase that we want to be much louder and perhaps the climax of the entire piece. We still set it up without pouncing on the last note of the previous phrase by placing a *crescendo* on that last note so that dynamically we have still set the listener up for something new. In this manner, we do not separate the piece into two sections but develop a sense of continuity. Remember, there are those times we definitely want to hear two opposing thoughts. ***At those times, you break the rule. We are trying to come up with rules that satisfy musical expressiveness most commonly.*** Another part of our job is to teach our students when we do not abide by the rule. The other thing we have to remember is that we are trying to attack the most common mistakes made by inexperienced singers.

For an example of where we end one phrase fairly soft but want to set up to begin the next one fairly loud and energetic, see "America," below.

Remember the television show, "Dukes of Hazard?" "General Lee" was the hot car that they used to perform their getaways. Picture for a minute "General Lee" in a chase scene, coming to a creek, but the bridge is out. In the approach to the creek enough momentum must be gathered to become airborne by the time the car has reached its bank. Think of the word, "sing" in the above example of "America" as being that moment when the "Dukes of Hazard" romp on the accelerator. Let the *crescendo* serve as the momentum gained by mashing down on the accelerator, the bar line serves as the moment when the car becomes airborne in order to get over it, and finally, the word "land" is the symbol of the car landing on the other side of the creek. This is how our intuitive students would appreciate us presenting the feeling of the music at that point. The thinkers would understand the *crescendo*, but this would even help them to not make the *crescendo* such a mechanical process. For the most part, it is more difficult to get the "sensibles" to understand emotion and feeling in music than the intuitives, especially if they are an ST combination. It is not as comfortable for them as it is the "intuitives."

An example of where we might want to make the singer conscious of beginning where he left off can be found in the hymn tune "For the Beauty of the Earth," when the first phrase melodically is repeated.

Between the words, skies and for, we take caution to begin the word "for" with the same dynamic level with which we ended on "skies." We then can immediately *crescendo* to make the second phrase different from the first and also begin to build to a climax in the hymn. The common approach would be to divide the entire hymn into two-measure segments with the first of the two measures being slightly louder than the second. The listener or singer then gets in the "hum-drum" mode of knowing what to expect and becomes very bored.

We lose a sense of anticipation when we know what to expect. Think about looking at the packages under the Christmas tree and knowing what is in every one of them. You may be anxious to open them Christmas day just because you like what happens to be in them. Now think about looking at all the packages under the tree and not knowing what is in any of them. The suspense definitely adds a degree of excitement. Music is no different. It always helps if we can stay within good performance practice but not quite give the listener exactly what was expected. Make the listener wait with great anticipation.

By examining the hymn, "For the Beauty of the Earth," we see that the redundancy of doing the same thing with each phrase destroys musicality. This brings us to our third rule.

3. No two consecutive notes or phrases should be alike.

It is so easy to fall into the trap of establishing what we want for a particular phrase and then making all phrases that are of the like rhythmic and melodic shape the same. Each phrase can be thought of as forming circles that begin at one dynamic level and make changes according to the arsis and thesis of the line. A new circle begins but must be connected to the first circle as was shown in previous rules. The sizes of the circles vary as we expand dynamic levels within the phrase. This is one way we can keep like phrases from sounding the same.

The text will always help us make decisions as to how we want to change like phrases if it differs when the notes and rests do not. What about repetitious or sequential patterns? We must be able to make decisions about where we want them to go. Let's look again at the canon. "Himmel and Erde." (All Things Shall Perish - p. 27) The sequence, "Music alone shall live," can be approached in several different manners. We could begin fairly loud and gradually soften each one or the opposite. These are the most common approaches. How about in the framework of a scenario such as this one:

You have asked your son to take the trash out before leaving for school. It is getting close to time for him to leave and he still has shown no inclination toward getting his chore done. First, you have politely made the request just as you would make a simple musical statement. On the second request, you have become much more firm and forceful with your tone of voice. On the third request you might very softly, but with great intensity say, "If you don't take the trash out, you may as well not ask me for the keys to the car Friday night!" Although the text does not change in the canon, this same approach could be made musically. If you think about it, the text does change in that we add the final phrase the last time, "never to die."

When thinking about not making consecutive notes alike, we have to remember that all notes are either leading to or falling away from something. In either case, it should happen gradually which means the notes will not be alike. Keep in mind as we begin to work with the other articulation rules, that the notes are always preparing tension and release by leading to and falling away from climaxes and strong beats. We want to draw attention to the shapes we are trying to make. Although this may sound like it contradicts what we said about keeping the element of surprise, this is prevented in the way we renew energy on off-beats, weak-beats in order to set up the strong beats or syllables in a word. Let's look at how it will work.

4. Place "lifts" or "accents" on weak-beats or off-beats.

Why do people like jazz? Would you agree that the pervasiveness of the rhythmic energy has a large influence on this? If so, how is that rhythmic energy achieved? It certainly does not happen with constant emphasis on the strong beat of the measure. There is a saying that "fine Bach is like fine jazz." Considering a lot of Bach's music is very instrumental in sound, even though the voices become the instruments, there is probably a lot of truth in that saying. Indeed, Bach's music must have rhythmic energy and drive.

Count off a measure of $\frac{4}{4}$ by emphasizing the beat and not the "and" of the beat: 1 + 2 + 3 + 4 +. Now count off the same measure putting more energy on the off-beat: 1 + 2 + 3 + 4 +. When you arrive at the end of the measure in the second example, you feel compelled to move on to the next measure, whereas, the first example makes you feel a finality at the end of the measure not encouraging you to move forward. This is what stops the forward motion in the music. It is what can make Handel's "Messiah" seem days long.

Remember, we are not actually going to accent the weak beats. We are only going to put a renewed "lift" on them in order to get to the next measure or phrase. As we examine several scores later on, we will begin to see that these weak or off-beats often fall in the text on articles, conjunctions, prepositions, and other places that serve as connecting devices to expand the text. We must also remember that the note that we energize belongs with what follows, not what preceded it. This is crucial if we are to keep the forward motion in the music. Without grouping the notes this way, the whole purpose of preparation is lost.

In various time-signatures we have the following possibilities: $\frac{2}{4}$ = the strong beat is on one, so the lift would be placed on two. $\frac{3}{4}$ = the strong beat is on one, so we have the choice of placing the lift on two or three, depending on the text and the syllabic stress of the text. As often as we can, place the lift on the last count of the measure in order to prepare the downbeat of the next and also to get across the bar line without interrupting the shaping of the phrase. $\frac{4}{4}$ = strong beats on one and three, so place lift or lifts on two and four. $\frac{6}{8}$ = strong beats on one and four leaving us four choices for lifts, two, three, five, and six. The most important weak beat to accent is the penultimate note of any phrase or cadence. *No phrase or cadence has a sense of completion without preparing it with the next to last note.* A little later we will look at several musical scores and see what our choices might be. We make those choices by first finding off-beats and weak-beats, looking at the text to narrow down those choices and finally deciding what fits best musically. At least we have given our students the guidelines to start making some of their own decisions. Now we teach them how to make assessments regarding use of the rules.

One of the things we have to consider when using our rule of accenting off-beats and weak-beats is how many do we use in a measure when several are possible, and how do we decide which of the choices is the best. Going back to our philosophy about jazz, we know that there is more energy in the off-beat than anything that falls on the beat. For this reason, if we have a choice between the two and the text makes sense either way, try to place the renewal on the off-beat. Also, if we have a choice where the only difference is one of note duration, always place the renewal on the smaller note value. See examples below. (The parenthesis indicate note groupings.)

The small note is often overlooked. It is not given much importance. We get much more energy and clarity if we pay more attention to the small note. It is not unlike paying attention to detail in daily life. I remember a colleague saying, "If you don't think the smallest detail is important, think about a micro-chip in a computer." Beautiful phrases are built out of taking care of all of the details. Anything beautiful has minute details that are often more beautiful than the whole product. They cause us to overlook the flaws.

5. **When a dotted note is followed by a note of shorter value, place the accent on the short note.**

   a. **Put a slight space between the dotted note and the short note.**

   b. **Put a slight *crescendo* on the dotted note.**

Again, the note of shortest value is slighted if we do not place special emphasis on it. Consequently, a dotted-eighth followed by a sixteenth note often is performed as a triplet figure with a rest rather than the three sixteenths tied, followed by a sixteenth. Count "one and duh" for your students as opposed to one ee and duh to show the difference as you display the following figures on the board.

one and duh   one ee and duh

The short note would belong with what follows.

By placing a slight space between the dotted note and the short note, it becomes easier to renew with the short note and it also is a clarifying factor for the short note. The slower the movement between the two notes, the less space. In a *legato* passage with a dotted half note followed by a quarter note, you would need no space.

Our sixth and final rule is usually used in the bass part and mostly helps shape cadence points. It also aids the young singer with vocal production. Actually, you will notice that by using these rules of articulation that many vocal problems are solved. The combination of articulation and good diction helps keep the sound placed correctly and the renewal of energy so infrequently insists that the singer constantly uses good breath support and management.

6. When the basses have a descending octave leap, put the accent on the second note and pull into the next note, especially at cadence points.

   a. Put a slight separation between the two notes of the octave leap.

Look at the following cadence. Play it on the piano first with no emphasis on the lower pitch of the octave leap **(Example A)**, then play it as indicated in the score **(Example B)**. Sustain all other pitches of the cadence so that the separation in the bass line is not so obvious. This separation allows the singer to "shift gears" and prepare the voice for the bottom register. Most young singers do not have the vocal mechanism or the ability to slur an octave leap in that area of their voice. Keep the bottom pitch as bright as possible so that the singer does not "swallow" the tone. The bright vowel will also produce much more sound with less effort. You will not need as many basses to get the same amount of sound down low if you keep the vowel bright.

Example A

Example B

This same philosophy will also work with the young female. So often, she approaches low pitches by singing way down into chest voice. Having her practice large leaps in the same manner as above will aid in keeping more head voice in the tone if the vowel is kept bright. If not, extra energy on the low pitch will only increase "chestiness." For both male and female voices, daily exercises moving downward will do far more to solve this type of vocal problem than anything else, as was discussed in the section on vocal production. You might also want to try having your singers sing an octave leap first by placing a finger on the forehead as they sing the top pitch, and then placing the finger on their chest as they sing the lower pitch. This will probably cause them to sing a very "chesty" sound. Follow this exercise by having them keep their finger placed on their forehead for both pitches.

On the following page is a summary or guide for all of the articulation rules.

RULES OF ARTICULATION

1. Never accent the last note of a phrase or the last syllable of a word.

2. All phrases begin where the previous one left off.

3. No two consecutive notes or phrases should be alike.

4. Place "lifts" or "accents" on weak-beats or off-beats. (penultimate note)

5. When a dotted note is followed by a note of shorter value, place the accent on the short note.

   a. Put a slight space between the dotted note and the short note.
   b. Put a slight *crescendo* on the dotted note.

6. When the basses have a descending octave leap, put an accent on the second note and pull into the next note, especially at cadence points.

   a. Put a slight space between the two notes of the octave leap.

In the next chapter we will examine several musical scores to see how the articulation and diction rules apply. Look through some of the scores for a more thorough understanding of how to use the rules. Once inexperienced singers begin to understand and use these rules, they sing very musically without any coaching from the teacher other than reminding them to use their own musical intellect. Sight-reading now has a whole new dimension. Make certain that the students begin applying the rules to their sight-reading exercises as soon as the first rule is presented. They need to develop habits of singing musically on the first reading of a piece or exercise. The articulation rules can be presented along with the very first rhythmic exercises you do in sight-reading, long before you introduce pitches.

Our main goal is to encourage the singer to become musically intelligent in his own right. Each step of the way, teachers must insist that the students always practice the concepts that are presented. It is a given that most students will not do anything that the teacher does not insist be done. The rules of articulation and diction must constantly be reinforced through application within the musical score.

This page left intentionally blank.

CHAPTER 4

"Elements of Expressive Singing and the Musical Score"

The intention of this chapter is not to say that anything presented is the correct way or the only way, but simply to present ideas for consideration. In several cases, optional choices will be discussed and why we might consider certain choices as making more sense musically. The main objective of the "rules" presented in the previous chapter is to give students a basis from which to make their own musical decisions. We want to make them *responsible* for singing musically at all times.

You will find as we begin to use the "rules" that it becomes much easier to know how to approach a score in terms of teaching it to young singers. Many shortcuts will become apparent in the process. None of this is possible however, until thorough score study has first been done. We will talk about that aspect of preparation a little later. Because the "rules" work much like outlining a chapter or diagramming sentences, we will find that we can teach most of what needs to be known about expressive phrasing of a particular piece by presenting one measure or a few rhythmic examples from it. Think of how much time we can save if we don't have to approach a piece measure by measure!

The focus of all that we have been talking about is on efficiency. In all of my years of teaching, I have never found anything that proved to aid in efficiency more than teaching the concepts of these rules of articulation and diction. Expression comes much sooner and the students are able to make their own assessments of what is expressive with much more frequency. Singing musically becomes habit rather than an ingredient singled out to be taught "once the notes are in place." For me, this has been the most time-saving avenue I have taken. But the greater reward is that the students are responsible for making the decisions.

They do not have to be high school students to use these rules. They can be taught and reinforced from a very young age. The very first introduction of rhythm is the time to begin teaching the concepts of articulation. Young children love body movement. Dalcroze eurhythmics basically use these same concepts because with that method we learn how to prepare the phrase through use of body movement and improvisation.

It is very exciting to see how much sense the music makes, and how simplified it becomes with the application of the rules. The hand-in-hand workings of the articulation and diction rules are fascinating. It is amazing to see how one functions with the other to solve inherent problems. The most surprising finding is the frequency with which the rules work the same in every style of music. Remember, it is all a matter of degree and that is where our expertise and experience must be used to make decisions. Subtlety is the secret. At first with our students, we will probably need to exaggerate, but then it must be toned for finesse and correct performance practice. We do not want the listener aware that we are using "rules" to create a beautiful performance. Without subtleties, we lose the beauty intended. We are back to a very mechanical presentation.

Although we introduced the Rules of Diction first in the last chapter, we will look at a piece of music in terms of articulation first. The diction rules were presented first in the last chapter only as a matter of convenience since they could be explained very quickly. Because articulation is what shapes the phrases more than any other factor, we will study our scores with those considerations before addressing anything else. Of course, text is one of the basic determinants for our final articulation decisions. As we make our decisions about articulation we will begin to notice how the articulation rules we use naturally resolve some of our diction problems, which is another reason we will first approach the score study in terms of articulation.

Let's start with some very simple pieces of music and see how much can be brought out even in the least complex of phrases.

Himmel und Erde (All Things Shall Perish)

1. Since we are in $\frac{3}{4}$ time, accents will be placed on count two or three depending on the text. We will place the accent on count three as often as possible because we want to use that last count of the measure as a lift into the next measure.

As you can see, that will work in almost every measure. The only place it will not work is where the word, "live" is on the last count of the measure. Because "live" is also the last word of the text phrase, we do not want to put extra emphasis on it. Now, look at the example below with the accents placed appropriately.

2. Next, look at dotted note phrases. We put the lift or accent on the short note that follows the dotted note.

We have dotted figures on "perish from" and "alone shall live." Why would we not use the dotted note rule on "perish from?" There are two reasons: one, the short note falls on the last syllable of the word (ish of perish) and two, we have placed an accent on the next note because it is the third or last count of the measure. (No two consecutive notes or phrases can be alike) In this case, we do not use the idea that we lean toward accenting the note of smallest value when we have a choice of putting accents on two consecutive notes simply because the short note is the last syllable of the word.

   3.   **We pay special attention to the penultimate note. The penultimate note of the final
         cadence is the most important lift that we will place. More attention should be paid
         to it than any other accent or lift we place on off-beats or weak-beats.**

We have two penultimate notes, one at the end of the first phrase ("from under the sky") and
one at the final cadence of the piece ("never to die"). Both should have accents, but there should be
more lift on the final cadence than on the first phrase. We can accomplish that by stretching out the
penultimate note on the word, "to," in the final cadence a bit more.

Finally, let's see how these rules work with our diction rules.

   4.   **Move all r's over to the next syllable or the next word as in the word "perish."
         It will now become "pe - rish" instead of "per-ish." We have previously discussed
         this. The word "under" would have the final "r" moved to the beginning of the
         word, "the." The same is true with the word, "never" where the "r" is moved to the
         beginning of the word, "to."**

   5.   Every word must have its own clean beginning. The most problematic words are
         those that begin with a vowel.

In this text we must be concerned with, "from under" and "music alone." On the text, "from
under," we simply are going to put a slash mark between the two words to remind us to be cautious
about running them together. (from/under) On the other, "music alone," by placing the accent on
the last count of the measure, we automatically solve the elision problem by placing the lift on "a" of
"alone." The accent draws attention to the word and causes us to pronounce the "a" of "alone" very
distinctly.

Now to use imagery for those students with whom it works so well, have the choir feel as if they
are reaching into sand and pulling out a long piece of stretchy fabric. Reach in on "a" of "alone," and
pull and feel the stretching on "lone." Have the feeling that you stretched the fabric into the "lone"
part of "alone." Pull with an upward motion of the hand or fist as you have the sensation of
stretching the fabric into that part of the word. This will provide a sensation which produces a very
legato connection between the two syllables of the word as well as an expansion on the strong syllable
of the word. From now on we will refer to this feeling as the "reach and pull" of shaping a phrase.
We always "reach" on the preparatory or weak-beat and "pull" on the strong- beat or strong syllable
of the word. (See Pictures 4-1, 4-2, 4-3, and 4-4)

Picture 4-1

Prepare to initiate the phrase (breath).

Picture 4-2

Pull upward into the phrase.

Picture 4-3

Stretch the climax of the phrase and enjoy it.

Picture 4-4

Finally, relax and prepare for the next phrase.

6. No two consecutive notes or phrases can be alike. Consequently, we must consider what we want to do with the sequences in this piece. We must first examine the text. What does the text tell us to do? Should each sequential pattern diminish, or should they *crescendo*? Perhaps they shouldvary as we discussed in a previous chapter. Do you remember when we asked our son to take out the garbage? When he didn't respond after the first request, we asked it more forcefully and with more volume. Finally, we stated it very softly but with *great* intensity?

In this piece our decision is probably a matter of personal preference.

You may want to experiment with your own choir to see the results of each before making your final choice.

7. Phrases should begin where the previous one left off.

In this piece, we have two places that need consideration. At the end of the first phrase, we must decide how to prepare getting from "under the sky" to "music alone shall live." That will depend on how we decide to treat the sequences. If we want the first sequence moderately loud with each of the following diminishing, then we will need to increase energy on the word, "sky," and *crescendo* into the breath. If we decide to begin the sequential patterns softly with each becoming stronger, we *decrescendo* on the word, "sky." If we decide to begin the sequences as if the first were a simple statement, we have to do very little to set that up. We would let the word, "sky," fall into a natural decay, take a breath, and simply go on with the next statement.

We have two places where there is a descending leap of a seventh. Although we are not going the apply the rule about the octave leap, there is something noteworthy. The first leap occurs in the first phrase. ("from under") By placing the weight (accent) on the third count ("from") the singer can lighten up the sound as he approaches the lower pitch on "under" and prevent a harsh, "chesty" sound. The tone can be produced with head voice. By head voice, we simply mean the upper register of the voice. The young singer can learn to stay in that register by singing more lightly as he approaches the lower pitches.

So now we see how the rules of articulation can even aid vocal production in more ways than were already discussed with the octave leap in the bass voicing. We will discover that this often is the case and that many vocal production problems are partially solved or completely alleviated by use of the articulation rules.

The other leap occurs between the last two phrases of the piece and really needs no special consideration since there is a definite break in the line at that point because of the fact that we have two different sentences that are separated with a breath. Because we have just completed sequential patterns and have reached our final cadence, we can take even more time with our entry into this last thought.

This is a very simple canon, yet, look how many things there are to think about. What if we didn't have the rules of articulation and we had to make all musical decisions, measure by measure? By saying, we add weight, accent, lift, (whatever terminology you prefer to use) on the third count except on the word, "live," we save a tremendous amount of time and mental energy that can well be used for other preparations. We have really picked this piece apart, but each time we use the "rules," it becomes easier to recognize how they should be implemented. Eventually, we develop habits that eliminate this kind of analyzation.

Let's analyze another musical example. This time, we will preview Bach's "Alleluia" from **Cantata 142**. Again we have a piece in $\frac{3}{4}$ time but with some hemiola inserted.

We will not discuss the accompaniment at this point, but deal solely with the melody line. Later on, we will see that we must use the same "rules" for the accompaniment as we do for the singers because it is vital to the overall best performance. The accompaniment enhances or detracts from the voice lines depending on how well it is molded to intertwine with the voice parts. If the accompanying figures are not approached with the same understanding as the vocal concepts, the piece will not "fit together" as one unit. The two mediums will seem at odds with each other although it may not be apparent to a less than sensitive ear.

For the sake of illustration I have used my own English text which I have taken from the German translation. It is not an exact translation. For the sake of saving time and space I have not included the rests which are in the original score to match the voice parts with the accompaniment.

"Alleluia"

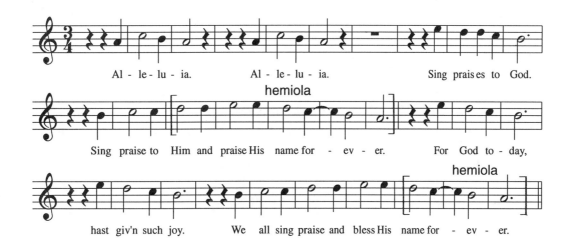

This piece has an introduction and accompaniment that is quite busy, almost entirely constituted of sixteenth-note patterns. For this reason, when the vocal lines enter after six measures, the entrance must be very solid. The entrance must be approached as if the singer has spotted a long-lost friend and is singing that entrance with the kind of greeting that would be extended to the friend.

In order to obtain this kind of excitement and energy on the entrance, place an accent on the anacrusis - the off-beat, pick-up note. (From this point on we will refer to the "lifted, energized, point of renewal, or note we add a little weight to," as an accented note.) The strong syllable of the word, "alleluia," is "lu." By placing the accent on the third beat of the measure both times that the word occurs, we place the stress correctly on the strong syllable of the word. The normal tendency is to stress the downbeat causing emphasis to be placed on the second and last syllables of the word, which breaks our rule about the last syllable of the word not receiving stress. Inexperienced singers will invariably land on the "ia" of "alleluia."

As we study this score before introducing it to the choir, it becomes apparent that we can teach the phrasing very quickly by simply saying, "renew on the third count except for the hemiola." This is indeed a shortcut to expressive singing, but will only happen once thorough score study has shown that a simple statement will satisfy the musical requirements of the entire piece. This is our goal. This is the kind of efficiency and time-saving technique we are looking for to allow us more depth in our teaching. Now we only have to practice the first phrase to get the idea of how we want to shape most of the phrases in this entire piece.

Al - le - lu - ia.   Sing prais-es to God.

Notice that although the rhythm of the second phrase is different, we can use the same articulation markings that we did in the first phrase. They will work for most of the piece. Renewal on the third count commonly works with the text.

Because we are constantly renewing on the third count, we must be careful to vary the amount of emphasis we place on that renewal or we will destroy the whole purpose of accenting weak beats. Redundancy will put us back where we were when we accented the downbeat every time. Remember, we are preparing the downbeat in the same manner that we prepare walking up steps. We must always think of that weak beat as a simple preparation rather than the outstanding feature. We will avoid mechanical singing by varying the amount of weight we place on the accented note and the attack with which we execute it. Using the text, "alleluia," as an example, make the attack on the first syllable a bit percussive to draw attention to the fact that the singer is entering now, after an introduction of several busy measures. The accent we place on the third syllable, "lu," is more of a broadening to indicate that it is the primary stressed syllable. "Sing praises to God," will use both accents with a more percussive attack with "sing," still being a little stronger since it occurs after a rest. By entering after a rest with increased energy we make the listener aware that something new is on its way.

In another edition of this piece the text at that same point is, "Sing praise unto God." (C. Fischer publication, edited by Charles Hirt) With the change of text in that edition, we could move the accent to the second count so that it falls on the first syllable of the word, "unto." This would vary what we have been doing and avoid redundancy. This would still place the accent on the penultimate (next to last) word of the phrase. We always want to strengthen cadences by preparing the resolution with extra energy on the penultimate note or word. Our other text, "sing praises to God," causes our accent to be placed on both the penultimate note and word by placing it on the third count.

Sing praise un - to God.

The hemiola is our next consideration. Hemiolas naturally provide points of tension in the piece. We want to keep this in mind as we decide how to attack the notes within the hemiola pattern. Because of the tension inherent in the hemiola, this is one time that each note has equal importance in building that tension. Because we do not have the tension and release found in most other phrases, we are going to stretch and broaden each note. Instruct the singers to place *tenuto* marks on each note of the hemiola.

Think of the hemiola as a "tug of war." Because of the ongoing tension in the fight to win at "tug of war," your arms begin to fatigue. At some point there is the need to let go momentarily to let the muscles relax a bit before developing a spasm that impedes any further endeavors. When you work as a team, as singers do in a choir, you can let go with one hand at a time to allow it to relax while maintaining your grip with the other hand. This gives the muscles a chance to regain strength. It is a bit like that in this hemiola pattern. We "pull" into each of the four notes of the hemiola ("name for - ev - er) gaining strength all of the way to our arrival at the "er" of "forever." Of course, we fade back on that syllable because it is the last syllable of a word and the last note of the phrase. It is a strong cadence point also. As we "pull" into each note, we maintain a very strong *legato* line moving from note to note, which is not unlike hanging on with one hand while we renew strength with the other.

Try having the singers reach out with alternating hands on each of the four notes in the hemiola and pull something in toward their waist. If they pull toward their chest, the high position will cause them to lose breath placement and energy. By pulling into the waist, they will use the lower abdominal muscles for breathing. It is important that the one hand keep pulling toward the waist as the other hand reaches out for the next note to create the *legato* line. Getting partners and having partner "A" pull one hand and then the other of partner "B" toward his waist is another way.
(See Pictures 4-5 and 4-6)

Picture 4-5

The student on the right prepares to pull while avoiding tension.

Picture 4-6

Notice the tension of the student on the left with double handed grip.

Because we do not want too much tension involved, there must eventually be a more relaxed motion than is felt with a "tug of war," or there is apt to be tension in the singing voice. Finesse is developed as the singer learns how to execute the accents appropriately. With inexperienced singers, begin with exaggerated sounds and then pull them back. At first, form jagged mountain peaks with the accents and then put a layer of satin over the top of them.

We have covered one aspect of singing the "Alleluia" musically. Dynamics will be our next consideration. We simply will decide where to put *crescendo, decrescendo* marks. On the first two "alleluias" it would make sense to crescendo up to the stressed syllable , "u," and then relax dynamically with the relaxation of the phrase. In this case, that *crescendo* also draws attention to the next accent. We will find that the phrases seem to make musical sense if we *crescendo* toward the next point of renewal (accent) each time and relax thereafter. This forms arches in the music and we then determine where we should place the highest arch (climax of the phrase).

We could consider the second "alleluia" an echo. This can be done in two different ways; cutting the dynamic level down considerably on the second one or performing the second one with a small ensemble. The ensemble could be placed within the choir or at another place in the performance site. If we decide to use the echo, this is one time we should break the rule that says every phrase should begin where the previous one left off because it would not make musical sense after the echo for the full ensemble to enter at that level on their next entrance. (Sing praises to God) The text of this phrase indicates more energy and again we will *crescendo* toward the accented note with an increased overall dynamic level.

When we begin the phrase that contains the hemiola, (Sing praise to Him) we will start with a gradual *crescendo* by using pulsing on each of the half-note values. Most of the increase in dynamics will be developed on each of these notes and at the same time, attention will be directed to the accented notes causing the revitalization to be more apparent. This will insure forward movement throughout the entire phrase and give strength to the hemiola as long as staggered breathing is used so that the singers do not take a breath in obvious places such as after the word, "Him," and between the words, "name forever." The *crescendo* will climax at "bless His name" with a little extra "sparkle" added to the word, "forever," but making certain that after the strong syllable, "ev" of the word, the final syllable is allowed to relax along with cadence resolution.

The sections of the piece that are similar to corresponding sections that we have just discussed will be treated very much the same allowing for some subtle differences. We do not want any two phrases to be exactly alike, so we will use the text to determine how we will adjust.

We deal with three-syllable words like, "forever," frequently. If we concentrate solely on the stressed middle syllable and not preparing it with energy on the first syllable, we lose vitality in the music. A prime example would be in "Hallelujah" chorus from the *Messiah*. It is natural to pounce with a great deal of weight on "ev" of "forever," especially since it always falls on the strong beat. Try putting an energized attack on the first syllable as if it is a greeting and stretching "ev" slightly

into the final syllable of the word. Follow the same pattern with the word, "and," on "and ever."
There is a new resiliency in the entire phrase. Instead of each group of three notes feeling like
repetition, each tends to build excitement which seems to be what the words intended.

for - ev - er and ev - er

If the word, "forever," is used in a slow, legato context, we would approach it differently. This is
the style of the three syllable word we are more frequently going to use. We still use the accent on
the first syllable as preparation for the stretch into the long syllable, followed by relaxation into the
third syllable. So, "we greet, expand into, and finally melt away." To put it into simple, concrete
terms for the sensible learner, we subtly accent, *crescendo* on the middle syllable, *decrescendo* on the
final. This may sound simple and very easy, but the trick is to get the inexperienced singer to do this
with finesse, especially the sensible learner who is also a thinker and may lean toward the mechanical
way of approaching things.

for - ev - er   mine

We must first get the singers to sing a three-syllable word with finesse before we can expect
phrases to have beautiful nuances that flow from one point to another. We find that we have to try
several different ways to accomplish this. A couple of
different imagery activities we can try in addition to
dynamic and score markings would be to have the singers
sit in their seat as if they are getting ready to run a race.
Greet the first syllable as if the gun just went off to start
the race, move slightly forward in the seat as the second
syllable is sung, and move back on the third (See Pictures
4-7 and 4-8). We also can use the paint brush visual by
grabbing the imaginary brush on the first syllable, pulling
it immediately across the board with the back of your
hand facing the board (bent wrist) on the second syllable,
squeeze all of the paint out of the brush, and allow the
brush to come back the other direction very gently as you
turn your wrist the opposite way. We could also picture
ourselves standing in water about waist-high. We see a
person floating toward us on a raft and just as he gets to
us, we push the raft away from us with our hands under
water, fingers pointed down using the back of our hands
to actually push the raft. Water is heavy. We have the
sensation of pushing the weight of the water away from
us, which in turn takes the raft and person with it. We

Picture 4-7
*Do not greet a phrase with this amount of
tension.*

then have the sensation of the water flowing gently back in place. The first syllable is prepared by
placing our hands under water, the second by pushing the water away, and the third with the water
gently returning to its original position.

Picture 4-8
Proper attitude toward greeting a phrase.

If you have not experimented much with imagery as a classroom tool, you may not only feel uncomfortable with it but even foolish. However, don't discount the results that can be obtained from it, especially when you consider that there are some learning styles that thrive on it. Statistics have shown that our music classes draw that type of learner. Some of these particular visuals may seem absurd. I can only share with you that they have all proven to be helpful in my own classroom. Obviously, some of them need more time to develop a sense of trust between the students before it would be feasible to try them. You have to be the judge of that with your own situation, your own students, and your own comfort zones. Don't be afraid to have your students laugh with you about reactions from some of the exercises. If we are not afraid to have our students laugh at us when we try to find things that will work, they will learn to laugh with us.

Let's look at a piece next that primarily is shaped with a three-syllable word much like what we just discussed, the "Kyrie" from Hassler's *Missa Secunda*. Again, we can teach expressive shaping by showing one measure of the piece and having the singers use the same philosophy for most of the entire "Kyrie." Look at the beginning measure of thematic material.

How many choices can you make regarding accents? First, find all the possible choices, then begin elimination. The next example demonstrates all of the choices. Do you agree?

Now lets begin the elimination process. The last accent on "son" we would cancel because it is the last syllable of a word. If we leave the accent on "e" of "eleison" we accomplish two things: one, we have our preparation for the stressed syllable and two, it gives the word, "eleison" its own clean beginning rather than the text sounding like it is supposed to be, "Ky-ri-e-e, lei-son." It is justifiable to keep that accent. What about the accent on the middle syllable of "Kyrie?" We have long phrases that only use the text, "Kyrie eleison." The whole text is composed of two, three-syllable words. Since we have only three-syllable words, perhaps we want a slight difference between them to avoid a mechanical or redundant sound. By putting a solid "k" sound on "Kyrie" and diminishing the sound on the other two syllables we notice more distinction between the two words than with our only accent on "e" of "eleison." Unlike many other three-syllable words, "Kyrie" does not have the strong middle syllable.

The example below shows how we would mark the score if we indeed did make the decision to shape the phrase as discussed.

If we looked at the entire score, we would find that much of it can be shaped with this same idea in mind. Look at the "Christe eleison" section.

If we think of the "Chris" of "Christe" as two eighth notes tied together, we realize how the two themes can be phrased exactly alike. In order to get inexperienced singers to sing the "Christe" with the flipped "r" of Latin, have them say, "Kuh - dee - steh" running the "Kuh" into the "dee" very rapidly.

There are no diphthongs in Latin. The "e" sounds should be said like long "a" sounds in English, but without the diphthong sound of "ee" at the end. The "s" on "son" of "eleison" should have an "s" sound rather than "z." Flip the "r" on "Kyrie". The student will have a better chance of doing this successfully after he has first tried "Christe" as shown.

One thing we did not discuss as far as rules of articulation that would greatly enhance the performance of the "Kyrie," is to tell the singer that anytime he has a moving part when other voice parts do not, his part should be brought out and the other singers should be sensitive to it. Of prime concern is the thematic material. Every entrance involving thematic material should receive special attention and energy. Practice a piece like the "Kyrie" by first having the singers sing only when they have thematic material. Next, have them sing when they have thematic material and moving parts that others do not have (shorter note values).

One of the difficult things about a piece like the "Kyrie" is getting the singers to sing without vocal strain in the tesitura that the composition calls for, especially tenors. The difficulty is made more apparent because it is thematic material of great importance and leaves the tenors very exposed at the beginning of the piece. They naturally set the tone for the entire composition.

Tell the tenors to try to sound like altos. This will encourage them to lighten the tone without it becoming whimpy. They will use more falsetto to negotiate the desired quality. If we teach them to start with falsetto, we can build on that to fill out the tone. Instead of beginning on the pitch indicated in the score, (usually the E above middle C) begin on an A above middle C so that the tenors are forced to sing falsetto. Have them sing with the altos. Once they learn to sing with a nice, light, supported tone in that key, move down only one-half step. Tell them not to change the weight of their sound. Keep it as feathery and light as it was on the A. Keep moving down by half-steps until you reach the correct key. At the same time, you must constantly remind them not to sing any heavier as you lower the keys by half-steps. Next, encourage the altos to sound like tenors. This will remove the "chesty" sound from their voices as they sing their first entrance on the same pitches as the tenors. The first measures of this piece have the tenors introducing the theme followed immediately by the altos on the same pitches.

We are seeing how many shortcuts we can take by simply outlining a piece in terms of the rules of articulation. There is no need to drill notes and get those solid before we begin to make music if we take this approach. By introducing a piece with one thought in mind such as accent on the third beat of the measure (Bach's "Alleluia") or introducing a piece with instruction on one measure to be followed somewhat throughout, we remove the boredom of pounding notes before we can do anything else and we teach our students to think musically at all times. If we first teach notes and then teach musicality as a second step, the students lose interest in the music and we waste an unbelievable amount of precious rehearsal time.

We are going to look at a piece of music next that can be outlined with four simple measures of varying rhythmic patterns. It is the Schumann, "Wenn ich ein Voglein War" ("Were I a Tiny Bird"). We are going to look at only the melody line since the voice parts are very similar in the duet. We will outline the piece in terms of rhythmic articulation with an understanding that we will have to make some adjustments for the text. By always beginning with the rhythmic articulation, it gives a foundation for the singers to sing every phrase musically and then they develop the skill of adjusting to the text as they sight-read. This also makes the singer much more aware of the text. By becoming more aware of it, they in turn pay more attention to good diction. Our rules of articulation *cause* the singer to be a more responsible musician (see facing page).

WENN ICH EIN VOGLEIN WAR

Wenn ich ein Vog - lein war, und auch zwei Flug - lein hatt, flog ich zu
dir, flog ich zu dir, Weil's a - ber nicht kann sein,
weil's a - ber nicht kann sein, bleib ich all - hier. Bin ich doch
weit von dir, bin cih doch im Schlaf bei dir und red mit dir,
und red mit dir. Wenn ich er - wa - chen tu, bin ich al -
lein. Es ver - geht kein Stund in der Nacht, da mein Her - ze nicht er - wacht
und an dich ge - denkt, und an dich ge - denkt, dass du mir viel -
tau - send mal, tau - send mal dein Herz ge - schenkt, dein Herz ge - schenkt.

With a quick study of "Wenn ich ein Voglein war" we find that it is ABA form with only four basic rhythmic considerations. We are going to discuss this piece as if we are presenting it for the first time to a young choir. Write the four rhythmic considerations on the blackboard as displayed below:

We will begin by counting each, but will divide them into two groups. First, count example one, 1,2,3 with the accent on three. Display the sound of the accent with the speaking voice. (1, 2, 3, 1, 2, 3, etc.) Next, count example two: 1, 2, & 3 (the note always gets the and of the beat.) Place the accent on the and of the beat. (l, 2, & 3, 1, 2, & 3) Now put the two measures together.
(1, 2, 3, 1, 2, & 3 - 1, 2, 3, 1, 2 & 3)

Add dynamics to the first two measures. We have spoken two sets of the two measures because the first two measures of the music are repeated as a sequence in the next two measures. We still are just speaking, but now add the dynamics with your voice inflection.

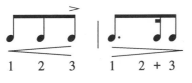

Now we will look at measures three and four. Measure three is spoken 1, 2, 3& with the accent on the & of the third beat. Finally, the fourth measure is simply 1&, 2&, 3& with increasing energy and pulse on each sub-division of the beat. When we combine these two measures, we want to save most of the *crescendo* for the dotted quarter note.

We combine the four measures in the following combination : (we are still just speaking counts with dynamics and accents)

> ms. 1 and 2 (two times)
> ms. 3 and 4 (two times)
> ms. 1 and 2 (two times) + 1, 2, 3, 1&, 2&, 3&

This is the "A" section of the piece. Practice just singing with counts on the melody line as you begin to read the music. Next insert the text. There will be some slight adjustments once you add the words, so let's look at the score to see where they will be.

In measure two, we cannot put the accent on the sixteenth note because it is the last syllable of the word. The fact that the students have been trained to watch for "lifts" on short notes that follow dotted notes will alert them to make sure the "small" note gets its fair share of attention even without the accent. (Refer to page 69 for the description of the "lift." We mark it as an accent, but it is a renewal of energy with a little extra weight being placed on the note that is to be the point of renewal.) This will aid in clarity and precision and make certain that we do not hear just the first and third beat of that measure. It will also help us to gracefully diminish into the last note of that phrase. The same is true of measure four on "Fluglein."

Our rules remain in tact for the next few measures until we get to measures nine and eleven. We cannot put the accent on the third count because it is the last syllable of the word, so we move it to count two, which is also a weak beat. Our rule for the dotted figure will work in this section and we are set for the rest of the "A" section.

Go back to measure eight for a moment. We will treat it as we did the dotted quarter note, 1&, 2& , 3& with a gradual pulse crescendo. We can also think of it being related to the inflection that Ed McMahon always used to introduce Johnny Carson, "He...........................re's Johnny!" The "He.........re's" is representative of measure eight, and the "Johnny" is the arrival at measure nine. This analogy will give the energy and breath support necessary to stretch the chromatic movement from the D to the D-sharp and E with good vocal production and musicality.

flog ich zu dir_____ Weil's
(Here's_____Johnny!)

One other thing we might note is the cadence point of the "A" section, measures thirteen and fourteen. Let the phrase relax, but make certain that we prepare with the penultimate note (all - lein). Stretch slightly and broaden the penultimate note, putting a little *crescendo* on that note so that it can *decrescendo* into the final note of the cadence. Have the feeling that the F-sharp "melts" into the final E.

Although we have placed *crescendo*, *decrescendo* marks on the first two phrases, they must not be alike. Each forms an arch, but the arch on the second sequence should be larger than on the first, increasing the dynamic level slightly and keeping that momentum all the way to the climax at measure nine. What we are doing is forming our arches with the *crescendo*, *decrescendo* patterns but constantly getting louder as we approach the climax, then on the sequence in measure eleven and twelve whose pattern was set in measures nine and ten of the climactic material, we hear the piece start to relax and wind down. The last two measures should probably be treated as a totally separate phrase (cadence) rather than being treated as a continuation of measures nine through twelve.

We are working with very short phrases in this entire piece. This is fairly typical of composers like Schumann and Schubert. Because they use such short phrases, we must find ways to make them interesting and connect to each other without interrupting the flow of the music. Even though we "make a separate phrase" of the cadence point, we still make sure it is considered part of the overall "A" section by holding out the eighth note on "sein" of the previous measure, for full value. We simply give it different character by entering in measure thirteen with renewed vitality and enhancing cadence resolution with our treatment of the penultimate note. As for the rest of the phrases in the entire "A" section, great care must be taken to connect all of the other phrases by making sure our "circles" or "arches" relate to one another. In other words, do not make an arch with the first phrase and completely stop the sound. The sound is "stopped" when three things happen: one, the last note of the beginning phrase is accented or given more weight than the note in front of it *(Articulation Rule #1 - Never accent the last note of a phrase or the last syllable of a word)*; two, the last note of the beginning phrase is not given full value as it diminishes *(Diction Rule # 1 - All syllables of the text must be held for the rhythmic duration indicated, on a pure vowel sound)*; three, the next phrase fails to begin where the previous one left off *(Articulation Rule # 2 - All phrases begin where the previous one left off)*. This is where our rule of articulation about beginning where we left off becomes so important. Measure thirteen, the cadence point, is one of those times that we do not want to begin where we ended with the previous phrase.

Although it may sound as if we have discussed a lot of information pertinent to the introduction of this piece, we can really simplify the information for our students as shown in this brief summary:

1. **Count measures one and two with accents**

2. **Add measures three and four in the same manner**

3. **Add dynamics first to measures one and two, then measures three and four**

4. **Line out the formula for how the measures combine to form the "A" section of the piece, speak them with accents and dynamics.**

5. **Sing the "A" section making articulation adjustments**

6. **Add the language**

After the students have tried to make the assessments on their own, we can bring in all of these other things we have discussed. It is important to allow them first to make their own decisions, giving their reasons. They may come up with ideas that make much better musical sense. We sometimes tend to overlook ideas because we have already formed habits.

Of course our next step is to see how well the "B" section relates to what we have discovered about the "A" section and we need to know if the return to the "A" section fits the first introduction of it. Again, let the students make the discoveries. Have them sight-read the "B" section on numbers. What are the differences and how much of the time can we use the same concepts as developed for the "A" section? Follow suit with the return to the "A" section. Insist that the students sight-read the melodic line of this piece once you have completed the rhythmic exercises. This is a piece that makes excellent sight-reading material for the young singer.

Now we will look at the "B" section (measures fifteen to measure twenty-seven) to find that the only time our articulation rules will not fit is in measure twenty-four where the sixteenth note falls on the last syllable of the word, so we ignore the accent in that measure. We might also give some consideration in measure seventeen to the sixteenth note off-beat on the word, "ich." We might want to put a slight lift on that note as well as the last count of the measure. We need the preparatory lift on the last count to help us expand on the dotted note that follows. We might also want to add extra energy on the sixteenth note in measure twenty even though it is not sung on a separate syllable.

The cadence in measure twenty-six can be treated in a couple of different ways. It does not resolve to the tonic of the minor key until the first measure of the return to the "A" section, so there is not a sense of finality at the end of the "B" section. We can either diminish to the end of the measure with a gradual *ritard* and pause at the end of the measure or we can take another approach. We could feel as if we were suspended on top of a bluff preparing to dive into the water below. The dotted note is our moment of preparation before we get ready to "plunge" back into the "A" section, so we hesitate on it slightly before we gradually fall into the three sixteenth notes picking up speed and momentum as we ascend into the return of the "A" section. If we do that, we must use the last sixteenth to "lift" us into the downbeat of the return (penultimate note). Experiment both ways and see which you think makes the best musical sense. It is important for your students to be flexible. This flexibility allows them to try different stylistic considerations.

The difference between the two "A" sections of the piece is in the text. The text causes some changes in the rhythmic patterns which means we must make new assessments as to where we place accents. The main difference is the use of two sixteenth notes on the first beat. We will treat them as we did the same pattern in measure seventeen. The off-beat sixteenth will receive an accent as well as the third count of the measure. The amount of lift should be slightly more on the third count than on the off-beat sixteenth because it is of more importance to get us "lifted" over the barline and keep the forward motion in the music. Remember, the other "lift" is mainly to keep the smaller note value from getting lost in the content of the rest of the measure.

The final cadence of the piece should be treated slightly different than the same material from the first "A" section. Because "A prime" is the end of the piece, there should be more sense of finality than in the "A" section. We can accomplish that by broadening the last phrase more, using a little more *ritardando*, and not letting the dynamic level drop this time.

See page 94 for an example of how the student scores should be marked.

WENN ICH EIN VOGLEIN WAR

*Students need to remain aware of the dotted rhythm. However, "chen" is the final syllable of the word and consequently cannot receive an accent.

Some pieces impose problems with articulation that we need to handle in unique ways if we are to perform the piece with good clarity. Handel's "L'Allegro il Penserosa ed il Moderato" ("Haste Thee Nymph") is a prime example. We will examine some of the difficult sections as well as how our basic rules aid us in stylizing and performing this piece.

One of the difficulties of this piece is that the voices are used in a very instrumental manner demanding extreme flexibility from the singer. Most young singers do not have this flexibility and even if they did, it still is difficult to achieve precision and clarity with more than a very small ensemble. Pieces like this are invaluable for what they teach. Not only is the exposure to the repertoire important, but the techniques that are developed from working with this type of literature are invaluable. We cannot teach singers to sing well unless we help them to develop flexibility in their voice along with other vocal techniques.

Again we are going to use the philosophy that singers cannot try to execute a certain technique by simply explaining what it should sound like, as we discussed when we talked about teaching singers how to sing a beautiful diminuendo. They must first experience the *diminuendo* to know what they are trying to achieve. So like we did with the *diminuendo* (pages 52 & 53), we are going to find ways to allow them to experience the form of articulation that the musical score calls for by using techniques similar to what we did with the numbers on *diminuendos* and *crescendos*. Once they have experienced the sound we are trying to achieve, we can daily continue our efforts to help them develop voice flexibility to perform the music without the aid of "gimmicks." This will not happen overnight. It is a daily training process that will go through several stages of development throughout the many years that follow.

We will begin by choosing various spots in the piece that pose "obstacles". For the purpose of illustrating techniques, we will make reference to the edition published by Walton Music Corporation, W7007, and edited by Geoffrey M. Mason (used with permission from the publisher). Our first examination will be of the reoccurring figures using the word, "laughter." Commonly, the rhythm pattern contains sixteenth notes in various groupings. At an allegro tempo, it is difficult to execute sixteenth notes without some degree of flexibility in the voice. The patterns in this piece using the word, "laughter," may be varied in several ways, each demanding the same technique.

Example A

Example B

Example C

We are going to use the numbers as we did for the *crescendo, decrescendo* process. Look at Example A. Have all of the students sing that example (measure 17 of the score) in the following manner:

Example A

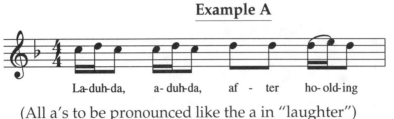

La-duh-da,   a- duh-da,   af - ter   ho- old-ing

(All a's to be pronounced like the a in "laughter")

Next, have just the "one's" and "two's" sing it as written in Example A. The rest of the choir, sing it as written.   Finally, for performance you may just want to have the "one's" sing it in it's altered state, with the rest of the choir trying to negotiate it as written in the original score. It is important that you have a different number do this the next time so that all of the students in the end, are getting the same opportunity to try to negotiate the phrases as written. In similar situations within one piece of music, you may not want to change each time it occurs or the students will forget which responsibility you have assigned to them in a particular measure, but make certain that in the next piece you sing requiring similar technique, you let other numbers do the false articulation.

We would treat **Example B** and **Example C** in a similar fashion, but with some variation.

Example B

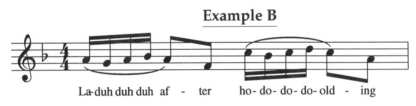

La-duh duh duh af - ter   ho- do- do- do-old - ing

(The "o" on "do" is pronounced long "o." The "a" is pronounced as it was in Example A.) This is what we would have the "ones" do since that is what they have done earlier in the piece. The "twos" would sing it as shown below:

Example B1

La - a - a - af   ter   ho- o - o - old - ing

The "threes" would sing it yet another way as you will see in **Example B2**.

Example B2

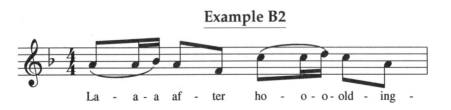

La - a - a af - ter   ho - o - o- old - ing -

The "fours" would sing as the original score is written. By combining the different rhythms, we have all of the notes covered. By changing some of the rhythm patterns, it removes the tension from the throat that is caused by young singers trying to negotiate too many sixteenth notes in a row when their instruments are not yet flexible enough to handle it. We will treat **Example C** very similarly.

Example C

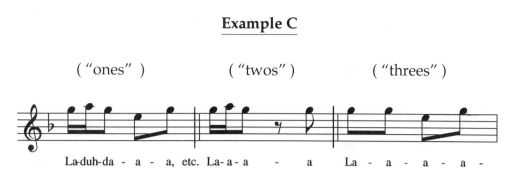

("ones")   ("twos")   ("threes")

La-duh-da - a - a, etc. La-a-a - a La - a - a - a -

As we discovered above, by leaving out one note, voice fatigue and tension will not set in as easily ("threes").

Look now at what occurs in the bass voice part. It becomes the "bass drum" that keeps the tempo steady for the rest of the choir.

Laugh - ter hold -

Guess what is going to happen here. Each quarter note is going to get closer and closer to the next one, especially since they are to be sung separated and staccato. The tempo will increase throughout this section as the other voices try to keep up with the beat of the "bass drum." We must find a way to fill the correct amount of space between each quarter note.

Have a section in the choir other than the bass section speak a percussive rhythmic pattern as the basses sing their part. The basses will begin to hear that rhythmic flavor in their mind as they sing. As the basses sing, have another section say, "Boom chick-a boom chick, boom chick-a boom chick," for the duration of the bass part in that section. You could also have one student tap that type of rhythmic "filler" with a drum stick until the basses are steady. The idea is to fill up the empty space with sound or movement that will keep the basses from moving to the next sound too soon.

The next section we will decipher is what I fondly call the "machine gun" section for the sopranos.

and Laugh - ter hold -

This is probably the most difficult spot in the entire piece to articulate cleanly. If you have a choir rather than a small ensemble, it is a trick to get this spot to come off well. First of all, you may not want to leave all of the sopranos on the soprano line. If you do, use the same method of articulation that you used in the other "Laughter" sections. The only place you will use alternate articulation is on the sixteenth notes. With the "ones," insert the "d." The "twos" and "threes" will alter the rhythm patterns so that the combination covers all areas as it did in the other similar example. This time however, insert an "h" for the word "holding" to prevent a glottal stroke that would occur if they just sang an "o." See the example that follows:

("twos")

and Laugh-ter   hold   -   ho,ho,ho,ho,ho,   ho,ho,ho,   ho,ho,ho,ho,ho,   ho   etc.

("threes")

and Laugh-ter hold   -   ho, ho, ho, ho, ho,ho, ho,   ho, ho, ho, ho, ho- ho -   etc.

This may seem to be more trouble than it is worth, but until you try it, you will not believe how much it cleans up the line. It will take a bit of practice for the singers to understand exactly how it works. The sensibles will grasp it immediately. With the intuitives, you simply tell them that the soprano part works much like the rapid fire of a machine gun.

In order to also include our original rules of articulation, place the accents where they are marked on each of the examples above to coincide with what our "fours" will do as they sing their parts as written but adding the renewal points.

Not only can we aid articulation by inserting tongued articulation with consonants like the "d," we can also modify or even change vowels to overcome difficulties. We often consider modifying vowels in order to ease vocal production on certain pitches in upper or lower registers, but what about modifying vowels in order to execute notes quickly and cleanly? There are instances in this piece where that will aid us tremendously. Look at the measure below:

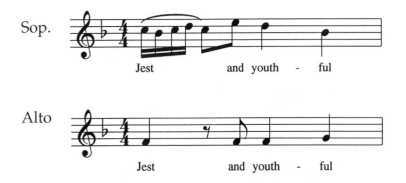

Sop.

Jest   and youth - ful

Alto

Jest   and youth - ful

The tenor part rhythmically duplicates the soprano part and the bass part likewise, duplicates the alto part. We will use the treble voicing to demonstrate our point and the male voices follow suit. Because the bass and alto voices simply hold a quarter note on the word, "Jest," they can sing the word with a good strong "eh" vowel, no distortion. The sopranos and tenors are going to use our four numbers again and do what they have been doing with all of the other sixteenth note patterns. "Fours" will sing it as written with one slight adjustment. Instead of singing, "jest," they will sing, "just." That vowel change lifts the soft palate more and does not tighten the throat as much. You could also try using "gist." "Just" will give a little darker sound and blend better with "jest," but experiment to see which way you hear the word, "jest," most prominently when the parts are sung together. The altos and basses should be able to cover any distortion of the "eh" vowel if they are conscious of singing a very tall, pure "eh" sound.

"Ones" will follow their usual routine of inserting the "d's" on the sixteenths for clarity. They must be conscious of maintaining the "eh" rather than the "uh" sound since we have already altered the vowel in other voices. (Jeh - deh - deh - deh - dest, not jeh - duh - duh - duh - dest as we did on "laughter") "Twos" and "Threes" will alternate their rhythm patterns as before:

Throughout the rest of the piece, we can use the same techniques for other words that impose similar problems. Most of the rest of the time, we can solve the problems by inserting the tongued articulation with a few singers. As often as possible, it is a good idea not to train young singers to execute melismatic passages, or passages like the ones in this piece, with the "h" in front of each vowel. This aspirate causes excessive air in the sound, a waste of breath energy, and teaches them to develop poor habits of connecting one note to another with an "h" inserted in front of the vowel. For instance, if the word, "Lord," is sung on two eighth notes, the singer will sing, "Lo - hord," instead of "Lo - ord." Practice using the pulse technique discussed earlier in this book instead of depending on the aspirate to perform melismatic passages.

The next step in "Haste Thee Nymph" is to remove as much of the tongued "d" and as many of the other alterations we have made as soon as possible. We may never be able to totally eliminate all of the alterations we have made, but we certainly want to remove enough to make them unnoticeable during a performance. In the end, leave just enough for a good performance within the abilities of your students and just enough for your students to know where the music is aiming. Let them experience quality.

Once they realize what the piece calls for, show them how to expand their personal vocal technique so that one day they will have the flexibility to execute the phrases as written with no "gimmicks." A good way in addition to vocalization to help them achieve this is to gradually remove some of the "gimmicks" like the ones we have used in this piece. Taking them all away at once is like never having shown them how to improve in the first place. It must be gradual.

The next piece we will study is, "Love's Antiphon" by Lloyd Pfautsch (published by Roger Dean; Catalog No. 15/1047). This piece is two folk songs introduced one at a time, one with male voices and the other with female voices. There is then a wonderful juxtaposition of the two, forming patterns of "two against three" and interesting dissonances. The ability of Pfautsch to "fit" the two folk songs together so well is exciting. There are rich tonal colors and many opportunities for the singer to "stretch" his "expressive wings."   The poetry is the familiar text by Robert Burns with the males singing, "My Love Is Like a Red, Red Rose." The females respond with, "My True Love Hath My Heart and I Have His," poetry of Sir Philip Sydney. The rich sonorities when we combine the two provides us with some very full, interesting eight-part singing.

There is a wealth of education in this piece. The singers will develop better "ears" because of what the piece demands with it dissonances and eight-part voicing. They will learn to increase breath management skills because the piece demands it. They will learn how to shape phrases beautifully and become very aware of good diction because this piece insists on those types of thought processes. Last, but not least, they will have a wonderful time singing this piece.

We are going to show something a little different with this piece. Instead of talking about each segment and how we are going to approach diction, articulation, etc., we are going to look at a score that is already completely marked. This type of marking should be done on the conductor's score before it is ever presented to the choir for the first time. If the conductor does not "know" the piece and does not know how he wants to present it to the choir, too much time is wasted in the little, precious rehearsal time available. We have already seen how much time can be saved by showing students a few things we can do with articulation in a given piece that will help them throughout the entire piece. In the next chapter, we will talk a bit more about how to study the score, but for now we will preview what this piece might look like marked and ready to present to our students.

On the following few pages you will see the entire piece outlined in a manner that will aid the conductor in presenting it to the choir. It is more helpful to use different colors of pencil for various markings, which we are not able to duplicate here. There is a code at the top of the music to indicate a set of score markings used for this piece.

> = primary renewal
< = secondary renewal
✓ = "lift" or *slight* separation
── = bring material out
⌢ = no breath
, = breathe

① A circle around any mark (see meas. 21) indicates a difference from the usual interpretaion.

② All like rhythmic patterns in all voices should be treated the same as the one marked.

To Henry J. Engbrecht and his choirs

Love's Antiphon
SSAATTBB

ROBERT BURNS
SIR PHILIP SYDNEY

LLOYD PFAUTSCH

4

6

true   love hath my   heart,   +   and | I   have   his. __   S My

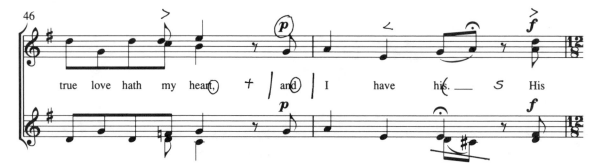

true   love hath my   heart,   + | and | I   have   his. __   S His

heart | in   me   keeps him | and me in | one,   N   in one,   N My

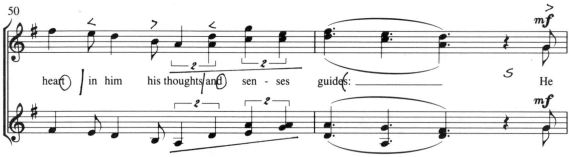

heart | in him   his thoughts and sen - ses   guides: _____   S   He

loves   my heart, for now   it | is   his   own,   N   his own,   N   I

11

You will notice that we consistently used primary accents (>) and secondary accents (<) within the same measure. This piece uses a basic rhythm pattern over and over:

(♩ ♪ ♬♬ or ♩ ♪♩ ♪)

If we make all of the accents equal, we are going to have very mechanized phrasing. The whole piece will become boring and lack vitality. We will lose the whole purpose of renewal, forward motion in the music.

By using our primary accent to lift us over the bar line and the secondary accent to renew energy within the measure, we can shape phrases more musically. Care must be taken not to allow *any* of the accents too much importance. They must have a soft edge. Make secondary accents more subtle than primary ones. Let the natural, strong beats fall into place and use the accents only as a "lift" into the strong beats or strong syllables of the words. The one thing that must be remembered is that **the accented notes, whether primary or secondary, must always be phrased or grouped with what follows and not what is in front of them**.

The first phrase of "Love's Antiphon" (ms. 1 - 4) would contain two circles or arches as we described earlier when talking about phrase shapings. There is one arch from measure 1 to 2 and one arch from measure 3 to 4. Phrase #2 (ms. 5 - 8) is similar to #1 but the second arch of that phrase is more prominent or "arches higher" than it's corresponding one from the first phrase. Phrase #3 (ms. 9 - 12) is different than #1 or #2 because it begins with a more intense sound (higher arch) and tapers or changes mood in the second arch, befitting to the text. (Excitement of noticing "how fair art thou" and then the sentiment of "so deep in love am I".) Phrase #4 begins with excitement again but that excitement keeps building on to the next phrase, which brings us to the phrase that is the climax of this section. The climax is emphasized with the change of tonality.

We study in terms of text and phrase shapes to make our assessments of how we will treat the rest of the piece. Obviously, the women's section has a whole different flavor. In the third section, where the two poems come together, we would want a third treatment of the phrases, with each of the women's and men's sections using a close semblance of the way the material was originally introduced. The mood is more serious as is implied by the augmentation. The section is more *legato*, adding more depth to the seriousness and honesty of the text. At first, each poem is sung as a statement or desire; here, we get the feeling that there is a commitment.

A couple of other things need to be noted about the markings in this score. Certain accents or breath marks are occasionally circled. This is a "flag" to let the singer know that they are deviating from a pattern that has been previously established. The check mark indicates a *very* slight separation, not a breath. Often, sixteenth notes are much cleaner and rhythmically more precise if we think about a slight space being between them and the dotted note that precedes them. The straight line is placed as a reminder that we should bring out material that differs from most of the other parts. In this piece, it also seems to enhance the tonal colors if the contrary motion to the melody is also somewhat more exposed.

For the sake of not cluttering the score excessively with markings, like rhythmic patterns are not marked separately. It is understood that all like rhythmic patterns in other voicings are articulated the same as the marked voice. You will notice that the diction is marked in this score, using the rules that were set forth in Chapter 3. When there are diphthongs used, it is wise to mark the score for a while as shown on the word, "I," measure 12.

Anything that can be marked for a time to break bad habits, is helpful. However, at some point the singer must be responsible for remembering good habits, without markings. At first we mark a score very thoroughly with our students. Second, we get them into the habit of marking their own correctly. Third, we teach them to become responsible, intelligent musicians without having to mark everything. One of the best ways we can reach this third step is through daily sight-reading, but only if we insist on applying rules of good musicianship.

One other thing to take note of in this score is the importance of the final penultimate note. The dissonance of the last chord is one of the most attractive things about this piece. I suppose one could read all kinds of things into the dissonance arriving at such a crucial point when the two texts combine to make their final statement. The penultimate note plays a very important role in setting up that dissonance. The "arrival" must be well prepared by that next to last note.

Picture 4-9

On count 6, grab the note out of the air using good energy and prepare to toss it to your left.

Picture 4-10

Lean body into count 1 following through with the toss.

How do we begin to teach this piece now that we have it marked? First of all, placing "lifts" in the strange places we have placed them (not on 1 or 4) is going to be so foreign to the students until they have done several exercises using the weak-beat philosophy, that we need to get them used to the "new" feeling. We are going to count 1,2,3,4,5,6 by placing accents on 3 and 6. After being able to comfortably count with the accents in place, sway to the left on beat one, toss your hands up in the air on beat three as if reaching for something to your left in order to "grab it and toss it over" to the next count. On four, sway to your right and at the same time toss the imaginary article that you grabbed out of the air to the right. Follow the same pattern with count six, moving to count one. Grab on six, toss and sway back to the left on count one. This allows the singers to feel the strong beat but also sense the preparation. It breaks the habit of landing so hard on the strong beat. In other words, we are developing skills of coordination which are essential to good singing and expressive musicianship. (See Pictures 4-9, 4-10 and 4-11)

Picture 4-11

On count 3, grab the note again using the same good energy and prepare to toss it back to the right.

In order to get the tenors to sing the tenor line with more ease, have the first tenors go to the blackboard, pick up an eraser and actually erase the blackboard as they sing. Next, have all of the singers pretend to be erasing the blackboard from their seat. Where the penultimate notes of each phrase occur or whichever note happens to be the accented note right before the end of the phrase, have them erase with a longer stroke. Erase with outward, circular motions to "feel" the arches of the phrases.

I have written the word, "sneeze," above the first soprano line in measure 38. We talked in an earlier chapter about how having the feeling that you are "sneezing" into a high note helps the placement. There are several instances that this sensation might improve the sound as the sopranos reach for the upper pitches in this section of the piece. They also need to be very "flirtatious" when they introduce their poem.

A great deal can be expressed solely with the text of this piece. The singers need to use a great deal of facial animation to make the text visually understood. The piece cannot exhude enough emotion without it.

We could go on at length talking about pieces of music and what we intend to do with them. For that matter, we could go on for several more pages just discussing this one piece. We are talking about a whole other book. The purpose of this book is not to examine anything with great thoroughness, but rather to "plant seeds." Hopefully, the few things we have talked about have just given some ideas that you will want to experiment with in your own classroom. Nothing marked in the "Love's Antiphon" score is necessarily right or wrong. They are just ideas to be shared and their purpose is to stir your own creative juices. This author has chosen a few pieces of music to demonstrate how we can apply the rules we discussed, how those concepts will make teaching a piece of music more efficient, this efficiency being important to allow time for a greater depth of learning.

Finally, how do we study a score in order to make intelligent decisions. We have talked about how we make decisions regarding articulation, diction, and phrasing. Now we need to look at the overall picture. The articulation, diction, dynamics, and phrase shapings only fall into place when we have the overall picture in place. We cannot decide how large an arch should be if we do not know how many sections are in a piece and where the climaxes are. This may sound very elementary, and perhaps it is; but, do you really know exactly how you want to teach a piece until you have studied it thoroughly? Did you know that you could teach Hassler's, "Kyrie Eleison" from the *Missa Secunda* (page 86) in an expressive manner by just showing the one measure? No, you do not know that until you have *really studied* the entire piece. That is how we save time in the classroom. We save it in the classroom by doing our homework outside of the classroom.

Thorough score study can be our best friend. Lack of it can be our worst enemy. All planning hinges and assumes we have first done our homework with the score. It is not enough to look at it briefly and decide it will "fit" your choir. We waste far too much time if we learn the score as we are teaching it to our choir.

Begin by looking for the different sections of the piece. Study the text. How similar are the sections? Finally, how can you narrow down the number of concepts you want to discuss or show on the board to

1. **Make the choir feel instantly successful with the piece (which instills the desire to continue working on the piece)?**

2. **Insure that the choir can do an expressive read-through of the piece?**

What can you tell the choir with the fewest number of words possible to start teaching them this piece? Where are patterns that will help them if they are made aware of them, ie. sequences, repetition, etc.? How much of the piece should the students be able to figure out on their own? These are questions to ask of ourselves when we are immersed in the study of a score. Once we know what the sections or the form of a piece are, how do the phrases break down. How many phrases are in each section? (This shows us proportionately how the piece is constructed.) Where is the climax of the piece and where are the climaxes within each section of the piece?

Now we are ready to start making more refined decisions. We can begin to decide on articulation and dynamics. We can determine how large each arch within phrases should be. We also take diction into consideration. Remember that frequently, elision problems are eleviated with placement of renewal accents. What are the best reasons for placing our points of renewal where we have chosen to place them? How is that set of choices going to bring out the expressive qualities of the music?

Once we have done all of this, we search for those choice few measures or the best example that we can use to teach the most possible about the piece. Next we decide if we do the read-through with text or numbers. We need to vary our approach to new material. The best way to keep a choir excited is to not have them be able to predict your every move or their own, for that matter. The bottom line is, "What is the best approach for this piece?"

The next step after deciding how to present the piece to your choir is to decide how you are going to conduct it to bring out those qualities. Here we delve into score study deeper. We memorize the outline of the piece by working up a study worksheet. Since you have a copy of the melody line of "Wenn ich ein Voglein War" on page 89, we will use that score to set up a sample worksheet. On the next page is a copy of how the worksheet might look.

A Score Study of "Wenn ich ein Voglein War"

sequence
A section = 3(2x2) +2 = 14 measures

sequence
B section = (2x2) + [2+2] + [2+2] = 12 measures

sequence   rit.
A1 section = 3(2x2) + 2 = 14 measures

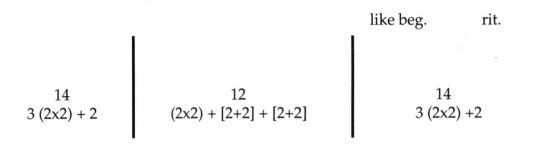

like beg.   rit.

14	12	14
3 (2x2) + 2	(2x2) + [2+2] + [2+2]	3 (2x2) +2
A	**B**	**A1**

This provides a quick overview of the entire score which makes for easy memorization. Now we decide what gestures we want to use to illicit the correct responses from our choir. See the copy of "Wenn ich ein Voglein War" on the next page to see how the conductor's outlined copy might look.

"Wenn ich ein Voglein War"

✓ = *changes in material*

* = *parentheses indicate slight variation of sequence pattern*

We can disseminate the following information about this score very rapidly from looking at our outline.

A section = 3 (2x2) + 2 Indicates that we have three sequence patterns.

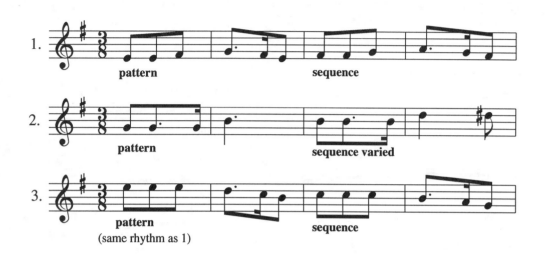

The (2x2) shows that the pattern is a two-measure phrase followed by the sequence of two measures; therefore, the 3 (2x2) shows us that all three sequences are formed with that same two-measure pattern followed by the sequence of two measures.

The final +2 tells us that the last two measures of the A section are the only two measures that are not part of sequential material. This makes it very easy to memorize the score in terms of the conducting gestures we want to use by simply deciding how we want to conduct each of the three sequences and finally how we want to end the section.

B section = We begin with another sequence (2x2) with the same format, (a two-measure pattern), the next bracket indicates that we have another phrase of four measures, but not with sequential material [2+2]. This is simply a four-measure portion of the B section, formed with two, two-measure phrases. That is concluded with a transitional section of four measures, again two, two-measure phrases; hence, our other [2+2].

A1 section = The formula is exactly like the A section. The only difference being the introduction of sixteenth notes to accommodate the new text. (See the outline of the score on page 125.)

This provides us with a very convenient study guide and makes score memorization in terms of conducting gestures a much easier task. We have also marked all dynamics on our worksheet, again to make us aware of suitable conducting gestures.

Obviously, this is a very simple score. This worksheet becomes more valuable as the complexity of the score increases. Learning how to outline a simple score will aid you in developing a worksheet for a more complex one. It is much like diagramming sentences, but guaranteed to make score memorization easier and probably more successful. It does not cause one to become mechanical with the music. It insures a knowledge of the score that will allow the conductor to become more expressive with his gestures. If one memorizes a score by simply remembering what the melody sounds like, many of the intricate details will be missed. The worksheet secures the ability to give preparations to the singers and that is the whole purpose of conducting.

This page left intentionally blank.

CHAPTER 5

"Expanding Your Personal Teaching Horizons"

We are ready for the challenge. We know how to plan, how to study. We have some idea of the differences in our students and how to assess those differences as well as how to address them in the classroom. We have found that there are ways to increase efficiency in the classroom. Now, we are ready to find ways to teach without talking.

The more frequently we can demonstrate or get a point across without articulating it, the more we will hold the attention of our students and save invaluable time. We must always be aware however, that being able to articulate something in a manner that is clear to our students is of prime importance. We cannot begin to demonstrate something that has not been explained clearly, first. Where we lose time and energy is when we keep presenting the same material by reiterating what we just said about it without finding new ways for non-verbal communication. The more we repeat ourselves with words, the more our students will just tune us out. We must be able to do more than explain something with words. If our students did not get the point the first time we tried to make it, they more than likely will not get it the second, third, or fourth time unless we change our method of presentation.

This is a discipline we develop within ourselves through a series of exercises. One of the exercises that I personally have found most beneficial to student teachers is to make them find ways to teach without talking. We start with an interval of one minute. They must find a way to teach for one minute without saying a word. They can work this into the lesson plan any place that they think it will make sense and work. We increase it to two minutes, five minutes, and finally ten minutes. These exercises help them find ways to replace talking with gestures, body movement, etc. What they discover is how much wasted talking they do.

The greatest benefit of this exercise is that it teaches the student teachers how to cut down on the number of words they use. This is perhaps the most beneficial thing we can all learn. If we can learn to simplify and choose as few words as possible, our students will remember much more of what we say. Another thing that the exercises do is cause us to be very conscious of our choice of words. If we limit the number of words we use, we want to make sure that the ones we choose, count for something. They must serve the purpose intended. Finally, we will get out of the habit of repeating ourselves so much. We all have a tendency to rely on repetition to insure our points are being well taken. All that we insure is training our students to ignore us the first few times because they learn to expect repetition from us. Consequently, we think the repetition is needed for our students to grasp the ideas. In a way, we have allowed them to train us. I recall one of our faculty members sharing a story with us recently. He had left the high school to take a college position. In the first faculty meeting he was trying to make a point when one of his colleagues reminded him that he no longer was working with high school students and he need not repeat himself. Once was sufficient to make his point. How true it is!

There is a difference in summarizing and repeating what you have said. Summarization often clears thoughts by bringing everything that has been said into miniscule form by using fewer words. For instance, we could summarize all the benefits of silence exercises this way:

1. **Teaches us to use fewer words**

2. **Teaches us to choose words carefully**

3. **Teaches us to avoid repeating ourselves**

We set up our exercises. First, we must plan the class carefully and decide where we can best implement silence. We will begin with two minutes, increase to five, ten, fifteen, etc. Finally, our ultimate challenge will be to teach **an entire class period** without saying a single word. Our rule will also include this: if we write any words on the board, we must say it in two words or less. Using any more written words than two completely negates the results of our exercise. We are trying to save time. If we begin to write everything on the board that we want to say, we increase wasted time because we could simply say it faster. Remember, the whole purpose of the exercise is to develop a discipline within ourselves.

To share with you from my own personal experience, I must tell you that every time I teach a full class period or even a good portion of a class period without saying anything, my students beg to do it more frequently. They are far more focused in that type of rehearsal than in any other and the rehearsal usually proves to bring us the best results. The first time you try this, I guarantee you will find it very exciting! The most amazing discovery is to find that it works. I also guarantee that you will learn far more than your students.

Earlier in this book, we talked about the possibilities of this sort of an exercise and we alluded to some of the things that might be tried. The exercise will not be successful until you and your students have established a rapport between you that includes a common language of gestures understood by all. This happens naturally in the day-to-day rehearsal. You conduct with certain gestures. You give off certain signals that indicate intonation needs adjustment, tone is strident, tight, dynamics are too loud or soft, etc. You are constantly communicating your gesture vocabulary to your students, although you may not be aware of it. Become aware by paying more attention to what gestures you use to illicit specific commands. What are the results?

In addition to gestures, we have other means of non-verbal communication. We can play the beginning of a phrase on the piano or any other instrument to indicate:

1. **where you want to rehearse**
2. **how you want to phrase**
3. **correctness of pitch or rhythm**
4. **which note is out of tune**
5. **what the typical phrasing of the entire piece is**
6. **simply, you want to begin class now**

As we mentioned before, this is a great way to get the attention of a large group. You can begin a non-verbal rehearsal by playing the first vocalises and immediately indicating with a gesture that you want the singers to sing it. You can go through all of the vocalises in the same manner or you could indicate the order by listing them on the blackboard along with the day's rehearsal agenda. This is information that has been placed on the board prior to the rehearsal. It is not included in our rule about writing on the board once class has begun, but it must be on the board *before* the class enters.

Another way you can correct pitches or indicate an intonation adjustment is to point to the pitches on a keyboard chart that you want a section or the choir to sing. This will only make sense if you have approached reading skill development through use of keyboards and/or keyboard charts. With keyboard work, you can correct wrong pitches by simply showing on the chart what is correct and then what they sang. Once the students visualize the error on the chart, they will not make the same error again. If it is a matter of intonation, when you arrive at that pitch on the chart, you can indicate with a gesture that the pitch needs to be raised or lowered a bit in order to be in tune. You can have the students then place their hand in position by allowing it to rest on top of their other hand so that the elbow is free to move up or down as needed to correct the pitch. We talked about this gesture in an earlier chapter. They simply raise the elbow slightly to "pull" a pitch that is flat "up" and they lower the elbow slightly allowing the pitch that is sharp to "relax" a bit.

You must also use facial expression to indicate your reactions to your students. You can let them know when they just made a wonderful sound either with your face or by using some sort of victory signal such as a raised fist along with appropriate facial expression. You can also indicate that something wasn't up to their capabilities with a slightly "disappointed" look. (an encouraging look of disappointment and not an angry look of disappointment) This is important in a non-verbal rehearsal because they are depending solely on your gestures and body language to know how to react. They are going to become extremely sensitive to every facial expression you present.

If you want to indicate phrasing you will introduce for that class period, have the example on the blackboard prior to class. You can then work the phrase and enhance certain phrase markings with your gestures. You can also have a few students sing and signal to others to join them using a gesture that lets them know that is the sound you are trying to illicit from all of them. We do not have to say, "Sing it like that." Most of the time, the students can hear and recognize what is sung beautifully and they have their own desires to copy it. We do not give our students credit often enough for having their own powers of intellect. We prefer to "spoon feed" them because we think it saves time.

If the students sing something we would like to change, with a simple nod of the head indicating "no," we can then deliver a gesture showing how the sound should change. This encourages the student to watch and listen to the results. Their ears become more sensitive to the results of their efforts, their eyes more sensitive to your gestures. By encouraging your students to use their own sets of gestures during rehearsals and by asking them what a certain phrase "feels" like, they give you an expanded vocabulary of gestures.

There are many avenues you can take to create a non-verbal rehearsal situation. You can see the necessity of good planning to make this type of rehearsal possible. Because it forces us to plan, the non-verbal exercise also develops that discipline. There are so many advantages to what we gain from a non-verbal exercise, whether it be for one minute or an entire class period. I encourage you to try it and I am anxious for you to experience the excitement of finding out that you can do it. You will love the response of your students! All of the avenues you choose depend on everything we have talked about in this book. In order to conduct a non-verbal rehearsal we depend on every resource to which we can possibly gain access. This means we are not only dependent on all of the things we have discussed in this book, but it makes us aware of how valuable it is to share with each other and learn from each other.

SUMMARY

Most occupations require some amount of research to stay active in the field. Teaching requires us to be students everyday that we are in the classroom. We must constantly search for new ideas and new methods to present the ideas. The more we experiment, the better chance we have of becoming master teachers. The material presented in this book is from several years of experimentation. Let's outline some of the points presented.

First of all, we need to find time for experimentation by becoming more efficient with our use of time. We also need to continue furthering our own education. Some of the ways we can allow time for experimentation are through:

1. **Good Planning**

2. **Teaching Sight-Reading**

3. **Narrowing Lists of Concepts**

4. **Using Gestures Instead of Words (non - verbal communication)**

Good Planning includes making thorough lesson plans once you have researched materials to be taught, choosing varied methods of presenting the material, and doing your own homework (thorough score study). There are ways to decide how much time you allow for each piece of music by categorizing the selections into easy, moderate, and difficult. By using a formula to determine the average number of minutes you have for the average selection, you can then double it for the difficult selections and cut it in half for the easy selections. You find the average by multiplying the number of rehearsals times the number of minutes in each rehearsal (subtract at least fifteen minutes from each rehearsal for warm-ups and sight-reading exercises) and divide by the number of selections you want to cover in one semester. From there, you develop your weekly and daily lesson plans.

Thorough score study means knowing the score well before you present it to the class. Know how you want to approach teaching it as well as how you want it to sound when it is performance-ready. Memorization of the score will allow you to concentrate more on the choir.

Teaching Sight-Reading includes skills using the keyboard, an understanding of these scales: major, minor, chromatic, and whole-tone. It also includes an understood of the intervals within an octave, both ascending and descending. All scales should be understand in fragment form as well as in their entirety. Rhythm is approached from a study of proportions; therefore, we will first introduce an eighth-note and present all other values in relation to it. This makes switching time signatures more easily grasped. Movable *do* seems to be easier to introduce than fixed *do* because the student does not need to have nearly as much information at his disposal to function with it. Fixed *do* requires knowledge of clefs, key signatures, and names of notes to begin to sing what is notated. Movable *do* can be read with a single line and three pitches. The young singer can begin to sight-read with much less information than fixed *do* necessitates. The intervallic reading of movable *do* enables the singer to transpose at ease and teaches the singer with perfect pitch to read intervals as well as pitches.

Teaching from the standpoint of the piano keyboard greatly enhances the singer's understanding of interval relationships, chord functions, and scale formations. By using the keyboard to teach sight-reading fundamentals, it is easy to transfer from movable *do* to fixed *do*. Because we live in a world of technology, our students have become accustomed to "hands on" activities. The keyboard helps accommodate their attitude towards needing that type of experience to maintain interest.

Narrowing the List of Concepts is an important attitude to take about everything we teach. We must constantly search for ways to be more concise. One of the most difficult areas to accomplish this in is teaching young musicians to sing expressively without being told what to do on every single note. We need to teach them to be **musically intelligent** in all areas. As was previously stated, the best favor we can do for them is teach them to not need us for their musical decisions.

We can narrow down the concepts needed to teach our students to be intelligent musicians by placing the qualities of expressive singing into three categories: dynamics, diction, and articulation. In terms of dynamics we simply show them how to establish the levels for a particular situation with a simple exercise which begins with a natural, energetic *mf* and relate each degree of dynamics to it, (i.e. *mf* to *f*, followed by *mf*, to *f*, to *ff*, etc.) We also can use a number system to reach extreme levels of dynamics that our young singers may not yet be able to produce due to a lack of development of their vocal mechanism. For *crescendos* **that occur over a long period of time, we number the students off in "fours" and establish when each "number" does its share of adding to the** *crescendo.* **Likewise, for the** *decrescendo,* **we decide which "numbers" drop out at what interval until they have learned to execute an energetic, focused** diminuendo.

Good diction and articulation can be promoted through an understanding and application of a few simple concepts or "rules." This is one of the most proficient ways to establish techniques of expressive singing. A chart of those rules can be found on the next page.

Rules Of Diction

1. **All syllables of the text must be held for the rhythmic duration indicated, on a pure vowel sound.**

2. **Purposely pronounce beginning and final consonants.**

3. **Every word must have its own clean beginning. (Do not elide one word into the next.)**

4. **If a word has a double consonant within it, sing only the second one and omit the first. (This does not apply to languages that require both to be sounded, such as Italian.)**

5. **Move all *r*'s over to the beginning of the next word or the next syllable of a word.**

Rules Of Articulation

1. Never accent the last note of a phrase or the last syllable of a word.

2. All phrases begin where the previous one left off.

3. No two consecutive notes or phrases should be alike.

4. Place "lifts" or "accents" on weak-beats or off-beats. (penultimate note)

5. When a dotted note is followed by a note of shorter value, place the accent on the short note.

   a. Put a slight space between the dotted note and the short note.
   b. Put a slight *crescendo* on the dotted note.

6. When the basses have a descending octave leap, put an accent on the second note and pull into the next note, especially at cadence points.

   a. Put a slight space between the two notes of the octave leap.

Use Gestures Instead of Words: This refers to more than conducting gestures. As we study different learning styles, we see the need to communicate in different ways. One form of communication is non-verbal communication. We can teach through different forms of imagery, some which include body movement, eurhythmics, visual aids, etc.

We need to constantly strive for ways of communication which illicit correct responses from our students, whether it be a response to a conducting gesture or a response to oral communication. The less we talk to get our point across, the better chance we have of holding our students' attention for a longer period of time. The fewer words we use for oral communication, the better chance there is that it will be remembered.

As we study personality temperaments and various learning styles, we begin to realize that it is important to find different methods of teaching. The most important thing for us to remember is that our students do not necessarily learn in the same manner that we do, so we must stretch our wings a bit to find ways to accommodate them. Our challenge is to learn to appreciate the differences, learn to find ways to teach those differences, and learn to draw upon the many resources we have with the diversity of personality temperaments in our classrooms. We may never fully understand the differences, but that is why it is so important to have time for experimentation. We must become efficient enough to allow ourselves the privilege of experimentation.

This book is called, "In Search of Musical Excellence." The author's intent was to present material that allows insight into that "search." There is no easy path. There are no shortcuts. Anything that includes the word "excellence" must also include two other words   "hard work." This book is about the commitment to excellence that one must make in order to become a master teacher.

There is no satisfaction like knowing that you have worked very hard to reach a goal. We take one small step at a time in our search for excellence. Each small step is costly but the rewards are immense. Sometimes the most difficult part of the journey is the time that it takes. Results are not attained overnight. Many of them are derived from an ongoing process. We must be persistent and diligent about our "search." We must work through the frustrations. Most of all, we must be *committed to excellence*, or the "search" will be futile.

There is no excitement in teaching like finding something that works and causes your students to improve. We can never fill our teaching with enough good resources in a single lifetime. The more we pay attention to the reactions of our students and the more we make a conscious effort to share with and learn from others, the more resources we will have. Developing our skills as a teacher takes great determination and self-discipline. We *expect* our students to take on those same qualities. Our qualities of self-discipline and determination are exercised in our willingness to experiment, read, study, share with others, continue our schooling, and focus intently on examining the results.

Each of our students wears a different mask. It is important that we try to find out what that mask is trying to tell us. We cannot possibly be all that we need to be to each of our students, but we can make the effort to try to understand each as well as we can with our own limitations. We owe each of our students the right to his individuality. We owe it to ourselves to maintain our own individuality. Each time individuality is constrained, resources are limited.

Because each of our students wear a different mask, we have the responsibility to find different ways of presenting material in the classroom. We will never be able to "reach" every student we teach, but if we do our best, that is all that can be asked of us.

Doing our best means we must do our homework, it means we must continue finding new resources, and it means we must maintain a positive attitude. Above all else, we must be willing to work hard and **allow ourselves to enjoy the results** of our hard work even though they may often fall short of what we had hoped they would achieve. Instead of beating ourselves down for what we did not accomplish, we must learn to focus that negative energy into something positive with our continued efforts to find new resources. Remember that all discouragements will be followed by encouragements if you are patient, determined, and willing to search for the signs of encouragement, however minute they may be.

We need to remove the word, "blame" from our vocabulary. It is not important to know who or what to blame for something not being right. It is only important to find a way to make it right. As long as we are looking for the "blame" we will not find the solution. We must also come to realize that we may not always find a suitable solution by ourselves. We must learn to rely on all the many wonderful resources that we have. It is not important to find the solution by yourself, only to find it. Sometimes that means we have to take a chance. The chance you take may not get the results you want, but it may be enough to lead you in a direction that eventually gets you there.

I encourage you to search for avenues that will add positive dimensions to your life. Those avenues will be different for each individual. You must find the ones that best serve you. Most of your colleagues want to be able to support you in every way that they can. Accept their help, their knowledge, their encouragement, and above all else, pass it on to every life you touch.

We all are richly blessed with the many wonderful friends and supportive colleagues that we have. Many of the ideas in this book are a result of my association with them. I cannot conclude this book without feeling very grateful for the rich experiences they have given me. Without their encouragement, their support, the sharing of their knowledge, I know I would not have enjoyed my many years of teaching to the extent that I have. I'm not sure I would have enjoyed them at all. I feel more than fortunate to get up each day looking forward to what it might bring. I know that there are many who cannot say the same. I realize that the people you work with can make your job pleasant or unpleasant. I am also fortunate in that regard. In conclusion I would like to say to all who have so been a part of my life, thank you for all the richness you have added to it.